Praise for *Fight Less, Love More*

"As a Harvard-trained family and divorce lawyer and couples mediator, Puhn is extremely well qualified to speak to communication difficulties in relationships. In this book, she outlines tactics to improve communication . . . that are simple to implement, remarkably effective, and will benefit couples in relationships troubled and healthy alike . . . Readers will gain a great deal from her contribution to the genre."
—*Publishers Weekly*

"Laurie Puhn hands couples who have lost their way a road map back to the relationship they want. Smart, empowering, and insightful, *Fight Less, Love More* offers real-life strategies for ending the cycle of fighting, hurt, and poor communication in which so many couples become entrenched."
—Rachel Greenwald, author of *Have Him at Hello*

"No matter how much two people love one another, at some point most couples end up in the same fight over and over, inadvertently stepping on land mines that trigger the cycle yet again. *Fight Less, Love More* explains how to step beyond habitual patterns and reconnect with the person you fell in love with."—Susan Piver, author of *The Wisdom of a Broken Heart*

"Laurie Puhn offers a no-frills book about how to have a great relationship. *Fight Less, Love More* contains brilliant and precise advice, the underlying implication being that healthy, loving couples are sane and smart—a sentiment that shines through on every page of clear, sensible information. I would recommend it as required reading for any couple."
Harville Hendrix, PhD, author of *Getting the Love You Want*

"Perhaps no conflict is more problematic for more people than that between partners and spouses. In this practical handbook, Laurie Puhn offers sound and pithy advice for today's time-pressed couples on how to deal with their differences in a smart and kind manner."—William Ury, coauthor of *Getting to Yes* and author of *The Power of a Positive No*

"Ever been in one of those here-we-go-again arguments with your mate, only to wish someone could step into your living room and sort things out once and for all? That's where Laurie Puhn comes in. *Fight Less, Love More* will help you cut through the usual stumbling blocks of your relationship and create positive and loving communication with your mate."
—Scott Haltzman, MD, author of *The Secrets of Happily Married Men*

FIGHT LESS, LOVE MORE

5-Minute
Conversations to Change
Your Relationship without
Blowing Up or Giving In

LAURIE PUHN, JD

RODALE.

© 2010 by Laurie Puhn

Trade hardcover published in October 2010.
Trade paperback published in October 2012.

Rodale books may be purchased for business or promotional use or for special sales. For information, please write to:
Special Markets Department, Rodale Inc., 733 Third Avenue, New York, NY 10017

Printed in the United States of America
Rodale Inc. makes every effort to use acid-free ♾, recycled paper ♻.

Book design by Joanna Williams

Library of Congress Cataloging-in-Publication Data

Puhn, Laurie.
    Fight less, love more : 5-minute conversations to change your relationship without blowing up or giving in / by Laurie Puhn.
        p.   cm.
    Includes bibliographical references.
    ISBN-13 978–1–60529–598–5   hardcover
    ISBN-13 978–1–60961–889–6   paperback
    1. Communication in marriage.   2. Interpersonal communication.   3. Man-woman relationships.   4. Intimacy (Psychology)   I. Title.
    HQ734.P959   2010
    646.7′8—dc22   2010031261

Distributed to the trade by Macmillan
4   6   8   10   9   7   5   3   paperback

We inspire and enable people to improve their lives and the world around them.
rodalebooks.com

To my husband, Dave, you are my best friend and the love of my life.

To my son, Blake, and my daughter, Emma, I didn't know what I was missing until I had both of you. I am so blessed to be your mother.

To my parents, Ellen and Howard, whose marriage provides an inspiration for this book and especially to my mother, whose vision helped make this book a reality.

CONTENTS

PART THREE
Change Your Thinking, Not Your Partner

INTRODUCTION

YOUR RELATIONSHIP HAS many redeeming qualities. How you and your partner communicate may not be one of them. By now, you've probably had more than enough pain, confusion, fighting, and misunderstanding. If you're like my clients, you may have reached the point where a lack of appreciation, respect, or intimacy may be threatening your relationship. The distance between you and your partner may seem so great that you no longer care whether he or she is home or away, coming or going, asleep or awake.

Well, I have some good news: This book can help you fix that. The 5-minute conversations and communication strategies you'll learn will help you create the relationship you want, or reclaim the loving relationship you used to have.

But before we move forward it's important that you agree to a few goals and responsibilities. In order to be successful, you must:

- Sincerely want to fight less and love your partner more. This means that right now, in this moment, you hold tightly to the hope that your relationship can and will be improved. You are ready to make your relationship your number one priority, if you haven't already.
- Accept responsibility for guiding change in your relationship.
- Agree to devote 5 minutes a day to practicing your new communication skills.

If you are able to enthusiastically commit to these guidelines, let's begin the journey to a better relationship. I will meet you where you are and guide you to where you want to be. Consider today the first day in a new, improved relationship!

So get comfortable and let's dig in. Our journey will include lots of revelatory moments that might cause you to laugh at some of the thoughtless things you and your partner have said and done. Or you may tear up when you recall the harsh, selfish, or hurtful comments you have received or made.

With each bit of insight you gain about your relationship, you will also move closer to a powerful answer to the question "Where did our love go and how can we get it back?" With that knowledge, you will know exactly which areas of your relationship you need to focus on to revitalize your relationship. With straight talk and practical solutions, *Fight Less, Love More* will help you stop your old, negative verbal habits and start new, positive ones. And as you set what you've learned into motion, you will be shocked to see your relationship transform before your eyes.

There is no guesswork involved here: The change happens right away. I promise that you will see results within the first 24 hours. You will create your own transformation and it will impact your mate immediately, influencing him or her to say and do things to continue the cycle of love that you initiated.

This book is equally relevant for everyone: young or old, male or female, those at the beginning of a great relationship, couples in the thick of it who know it could be better, and even those who feel that there is no hope left for their relationship. No matter who you are or where your relationship falls on this spectrum, a more satisfying, reenergized love awaits you.

Start reading. Start learning. Start doing.

And expect a new beginning.

PART ONE

CRACKING THE CODE TO RELATIONSHIP BLISS

YOU CAN DO IT!

IN THE BEGINNING, when your love was new, you probably thought your mate was the best thing that had ever happened to you. You couldn't get enough of each other. You both felt valued, appreciated, and loved. Even your friends and families commented on what a wonderful couple you made. But something seems to have happened to your perfect match. Your mate treats you with less respect and consideration than he used to—less than he shows friends and colleagues. Frustration and anger often creep into your conversations, and the next thing you know, you're fighting. Again. You know that you are both good people and that you love one another, but somehow you have ended up in a bad relationship. Where did it all go wrong?

Until now, you may have been hoping that your relationship would turn around on its own. But we both know that won't happen. There will be no turnaround until one of you identifies the problem and takes steps toward resolving it. And since you're the one with the book in your hands, you'll need to be the first person to own that responsibility.

If you want a better relationship tomorrow, the work begins today. It's time to do something wonderful for yourself, your partner, and your relationship. There are no more "buts" about it!

Excuse #1: But . . . It's Too Late

If this excuse resonates with you, you're probably thinking, "I'm worried we're too far gone. We can't turn this thing around. Maybe we're just destined to be unhappy. Maybe we should never have gotten together in the first place." Those are all excuses that take the pressure off you. After all, why try to fix something that is beyond repair?

But here's the thing: Even the best couples fall into bad relationship habits. Most of us just want to love and be loved. We want relationships filled with respect and appreciation as well as passion. Yet we've never been taught the verbal skills we need to use to give and get that kind of love. Without this training, in our noble pursuit of that love, we say and do things that cause the opposite to happen. We one-up each other, poke and prod about flaws, and demand the last word. We make thoughtless word choices that come back to haunt us. We unintentionally (and sometimes intentionally) turn conversations into conflicts. We yell and scream in our quest for love, or we do just the opposite— give in and hold in our feelings to avoid arguments.

Today, you will obtain a new lens through which to view your relationship and your conversations with your mate. This lens will help you to see clearly the weak verbal habits that are sabotaging your relationship. You'll also receive the tools you need to restructure your words so you can rebuild your love. You will become a better person and a better role model for your children. Be hopeful—your best days are right in front of you!

My uncle Joe's experience with dieting offers a stark illustration of how incorrect information and a lack of awareness can block someone from getting what he wants. Joe, who has been overweight all his life and hardly ever diets, had attempted a diet for 2 weeks and was upset because he had lost only 2 pounds. "What are you eating?" I asked him. "A lot of salads and chicken and no desserts," he said. That seemed like a reasonable plan. "What kinds of salads do you eat?" I asked. I was shocked when he told me, "I eat Caesar salad, Cobb salad, things like that, with my chicken. You know, the basics." There it was. Joe couldn't lose weight because he didn't know which salads were low calorie. Similarly, most couples I work with simply don't know which verbal skills work for them and which work against them. For example, one spouse might think that dispensing advice like "It's cold outside, you need a jacket," "You should join a gym," or "Here's what you should say to your boss" shows love and connection. Yet in reality, offering unwanted advice can be a verbal disaster that breeds resentment.

Every couple has difficult issues to manage. We all face challenges like managing money, making difficult decisions, raising children, caring for aging parents, and maintaining a household. But it's the couples who are able to communicate with one another who weather the rough patches. It's never too late to raise your awareness and change your words to change your relationship.

Excuse #2: But . . . Don't We Need Therapy?

Most of us think that a couple in crisis needs counseling to "work out issues." But research shows that more than two-thirds of couples who attend relationship counseling are no better off after 1 year of therapy than they were when they walked in their therapist's door. Clearly, then, therapy is not a cure-all for ending marital strife.

The years I've spent mediating couple disputes and marital problems have taught me that most marital conflicts stem not from emotional problems but from weak communication skills. With the exception of couples who are facing very serious, life-threatening issues such as addiction, mental illness, or abuse (which call for specific mental health therapies), the solution for almost everyone else I've encountered is improved communication skills.

Why isn't therapy the answer? Therapy is designed to explore your emotions, to dig deep into the past and tug at your rough edges to discover the source of your relationship problems. Often it leads only to the rehashing of past hurts and leaves couples with more questions and no answers. If you're like most people, there is nothing wrong with you *and* there is nothing wrong with your mate (you may not believe me now, but you will by the end of this book!). What you need is information and tools to fight less and love more. Even if your mate stubbornly refuses to change, you can improve your own verbal skills so that your mate begins to hear what you say and know what you mean.

What you are probably experiencing are conversational struggles, not people struggles, and conversational struggles can be resolved with *Fight Less, Love More*. When we view marital problems as conversational problems rather than people problems, we see that our dilemmas do not stem from deep-seated emotional flaws, but rather from communication flaws that are easy to weed out.

Excuse #3: But . . . We're Too Different

News flash: Every person is different! Each of us has unique preferences and ideas about most things, from trivial matters like what toppings you like on your pizza to big life decisions like how to raise your children. Getting married and going from "me" to "we" does not automatically eliminate those differences between partners. In fact, an individual's own preferences also change from year to year, so it follows that two people will continue to develop *new* differences as time goes on. That means that if you want a happy marriage that's built to last, you're going to need to know how to negotiate and communicate about a wide variety of differences.

A major study compared two groups of couples, those who married between 1964 and 1980 and those who married between 1981 and 1997. The latter group reported *significantly* higher levels of conflict and lower levels of marital interaction (meaning that they spent less time together doing things like enjoying a meal, shopping, visiting friends, working on projects around the house, and going out for entertainment). From my observations, interviews, and mediation work with couples, it's my opinion that during the last decade the number of couples in conflict has increased. Even couples married just a few years are spending little time interacting with each other, and when they come into my office, they carry extremely long lists of battle topics.

We fight more today because we have ambiguous gender roles, additional work/life balance stressors, and more opportunities for differences of opinion and disagreements. Years ago, when a majority of mothers stayed at home, couples may have fought about how to spend money, but they were less likely to fight about who should be responsible for earning the family income and who should shoulder the responsibilities of child care and household chores. Today, approximately 70 percent of mothers of children under the age of 18 are in the labor force. Recent research has shed light on a surprising trend: Many married people believe that they undertake a larger share of the housework than they actually do. When it comes time to negotiate housework and both people overestimate how much they already contribute, how can the negotiation *not* lead to a fight?

HAVE YOU HEARD?

An MSNBC poll asked whether household chores were shared or done by just one person. Seventy-four percent of men said household chores were shared, while only 51 percent of women said chores were shared.

Fueled by our country's economic growth over the past 35 years, we have more purchasing choices than ever before, from what kind of toothpaste to buy (fluoride, tartar control, extra whitening, or all three!) to what kind of computer, cell phone, or television to get. Though you would think that having so many choices would make us happier, research shows that having too many choices is counterproductive, making us stressed out and anxious about the options we had to pass up. And of course, all of these choices provide additional opportunities to argue with our partners.

Nowadays, thanks to no-fault divorces and do-it-yourself legal filing, it's easier than ever to end a marriage. With about one in five marriages ending before the fifth anniversary, it's clear that when marital discord surfaces, many people jump ship to look for someone who is "more compatible." Yet divorce rates for second (and third) marriages are even higher than they are for first marriages. Simply choosing a different partner doesn't mean that you'll never have a disagreement again. The only way to navigate around naturally occurring differences in perspectives, personalities, and preferences is to change your mind-set and communication strategies—not your partner. You can become empowered with the verbal skills that will allow you to resolve any difference, at any time, with anyone.

Excuse #4: But . . . It's Too Hard

Are the 5-minute conversations in this book hard to use? No way! After you spend some time reading and reviewing the lessons in this book, all you have to do is use the five vital manners discussed in Chapter 3 every day and add on the other 5-minute conversations that will help to prevent or resolve new and ongoing stressful situations between you and your partner.

How will you know which 5-minute conversation to choose? After a while, it will be easy to know which strategy is the best fit for a given situation. For example, if you want more appreciation in your relationship, then use the conversation in Chapter 5 (Inspire Appreciation: End Relationship Madness). If you want your mate to open up to you, use the conversation in Chapter 8 (Awaken Your Silent Mate: Pump Up a Verbal Exchange). If nothing bothers you on a given day, then just stick to the five vital manners, required daily, which reinforce the foundation of lasting love.

After a few uses of the 5-minute conversations, your partner won't withdraw or feel threatened by hearing the words "let's have a 5-minute conversation" because he or she will know that the talk will end shortly, without a fight. Both of you will begin to like these simple conversations that quickly solve problems. You will discover how easy it is for both of you to move from complaining to explaining, from rejecting to accepting, from conspiring to admiring, and from alienation to reconciliation.

In 5 minutes you will see results: a fight avoided, a decision made, an apology given, a word of appreciation spoken. Use these strategies and you'll ignite a new mood of respect, cooperation, and love.

Excuse #5: But . . . My Partner Won't Participate

I know you may be wondering, "How can anything change if I read this book and my partner doesn't?" Trust me, your relationship will change. It's a chain reaction. In relationships, when one person makes a change in the words he or she uses, the other person will be influenced to respond in a different way. If you say, "I can't believe you lost your keys again," you know you'll trigger a defensive response such as "What? Like you've never lost your keys." But if you say, "That's too bad you misplaced your keys. Can I help you look for them?" you'll trigger a different, more appreciative response. Once you have the right words to use in a 5-minute conversation, it's easy to predict the effects they will have. That means you have the power to influence the way your partner responds to you—good, bad, or indifferent.

If both of you read and use this book, then the results will be even more visible, the changes more dramatic. Working together for a common goal is always better—and after all, logically, both of you should want to fight less and love more. But even if your partner isn't on board, you can still restructure *your* side of your conversations to create change. You can become a great partner who has the power to make a great relationship. You see, it takes two people to start an argument, but only one to end it.

Excuse #6: I'm Not Sure I Can Do It Alone

You are not alone! Just as you wouldn't embark upon an unknown path without a map and a guide, I am your guide on this journey, and you are holding the map. With it, you won't get lost. It's up to you to do the work every day, but you will have support every step of the way.

Whether you're beginning to build a life together, stuck in a years-long relationship rut, or teetering on the brink of divorce, it's never too late or too early to learn the tools to bring unity, joy, and more love to your relationship.

LOVE IS CONDITIONAL

AS A HARVARD-TRAINED lawyer, mediator, and relationship expert, I've worked with countless couples and individuals who needed help reaching agreements and keeping their marriages afloat. Time and again, my clients and audiences have turned to me for quick and simple conflict resolution strategies and love-building skills to manage the emotionally charged, up close, and difficult conversations they were having with their loved ones.

My action-oriented plan was developed through years of research, experimentation, and observation. Plus, during my dating years, I experienced my own share of emotional flare-ups with boyfriends, and even now as a wife and mother, I am not immune to the occasional senseless fights and fleeting feelings of anger toward my husband. But what sets my relationship apart from those that go downhill and struggle to survive are the communication skills I can pull out of my back pocket when trouble is brewing. My plan is to equip you with those same skills. Those skills revolve around a set of 5-minute conversations I developed for my clients to use in the comfort of their homes. The plan isn't only to have you fight less, because you can do that by just keeping your opinions to yourself and letting your mate walk all over you. That results in no fight, but also no love. This innovative plan gives you an assertive way to fight that actually increases the love you and your partner feel for one another. The compact strategy for change is based on three fundamental guiding principles:

1. Love is conditional.
2. Love's conditions are met by using the right verbal skills.
3. Couples don't have to talk *more*, they have to talk *better*.

Principle #1: Love Is Conditional

"Wait a second," you're probably thinking, "isn't love supposed to be *un*conditional?" You're not alone in thinking this—many of us are brought up to believe that romantic love should survive "no matter what." After talking to thousands of couples in crisis, it's become clear to me that this belief is one of the biggest saboteurs of relationship success. People who believe that love conquers all and that our mates should love us unconditionally in the same way that we love our children are setting themselves up for a total marriage meltdown. When love fails to meet those lofty expectations—as it inevitably will—people become disillusioned ("How could this have happened?"), resentful ("But he promised to love me forever!"), and angry ("I deserve better than this!").

You see, there *are* essential conditions that must be met for mature love to survive and thrive. When those conditions are not met, love evaporates and fighting increases. Every person in the world should expect the love in his or her relationship to disintegrate if the conditions for love aren't kept alive. What are those essential conditions? They are the things every human being needs and wants: appreciation, respect, compassion, trust, and companionship. To have a happy and satisfying relationship, we must actively and purposefully say and do things, each and every day, to create and sustain these conditions. If we instead continue to believe that love is unconditional and we shouldn't have to make any special effort to keep it alive, then love is doomed. It's that simple.

Principle #2: Love's Conditions Are Met by Using the Right Verbal Skills

Did you know that nearly every comment you make conveys respect or disrespect, appreciation or indifference, compassion or criticism, trust or betrayal, and companionship or isolation? To emphasize the positive values instead of the negative ones takes skillful communication. We must become aware of any weak communication habits we have and replace them with strong verbal skills. And verbal promises or commitments must be backed by action. You don't have to accept the current state of your relationship as inevitable. You have the power to take charge and create the conditions for stronger, lasting love, one conversation at a time.

Principle #3: Couples Don't Have to Talk *More,* They Have to Talk *Better*

Many psychologists hold the conventional idea that a successful marriage depends on spending more time communicating, but in my opinion, this is seriously outdated. In our high-tech, multi-tasking, dual-earner society, busy couples simply don't have the time or money for weekend getaways and weekly counseling, nor do they have any interest in having long daily conversations after a long day at work or once the kids go to bed. Even if they do, it's hard to commit to a relationship improvement plan that may take months or years to produce results. And when couples with poor communication skills do talk more, sometimes their problems only grow worse. Today's couples will not find success by spending more time communicating with each other, but rather by using their limited time to talk *better*.

Aligning the Three Principles: The 5-Minute Conversation

My husband tells me that while hearing "Honey, we have to talk" immediately raises his blood pressure, my saying "Honey, can we have a 5-minute conversation?" actually makes him feel better because he knows that whatever issue it is that we're confronting will be resolved in 5 minutes. You are about to learn a new way of communicating that will give you astounding results in minutes by taking away your urge to be judgmental, accusatory, and right at all costs. You will engage in easy, step-by-step conversations that will keep you and your partner focused on sharing information and will move the conversation forward from problem to solution with no detours. I guarantee that after just a few days of practice, you will start to see and feel results.

How can you create the conditions for love to exist in only 5 minutes a day? Each 5-minute conversation will result in an instant positive response from your mate: a smile, a thank-you, a soft touch, a compliment, a few words of understanding, appreciation, a compromise, or simply an overall sense that you've been heard and valued. This rewarding payoff will motivate you to keep going with your new communication strategy. Just as you wake up every day, brush your teeth, and get dressed, these 5-minute conversations will become part of your daily routine. If you flex your relationship muscles every day, you will make your relationship stronger.

❤ ❤ ❤

I've shared the conversations and mediation strategies in this book with thousands of people at my public-speaking events, as well as with hundreds of individuals and couples in my practice who have been surprised and thrilled by the quick turnaround they've seen in their love lives. If you're ready for a real change that eliminates angry silences, character assassinations, slammed doors, breakups, and even divorce, then you have the right book in your hands. In less time than it takes to drink a cup of coffee, you can take action to change your relationship.

PART TWO

5 MINUTES TO FIGHT LESS AND LOVE MORE

3

TAME RUDENESS: INSTALL A DAILY COMMUNICATION ROUTINE

The greatest discovery of all time is that a person can change his future by merely changing his attitude.

—OPRAH WINFREY

Once upon a time, there was a clear distinction between rudeness and polite, considerate behavior. People knew when to say "excuse me," "I'm sorry," and "thank you," and closing a door in someone's face, knocking into a stranger on the street, and forgetting to return a phone call were not acceptable. But these days, a new kind of rudeness is on the rise. And the worst thing is that people don't even realize they're doing it.

Today's "new rude" behaviors stem from neglect, a lack of appreciation, and a lack of awareness. From the multitasker with no time to spare to the technocentric person with rude cell phone, e-mail, and text-messaging habits, certain impolite and disrespectful behaviors have been labeled efficient, necessary, and normal. And of course, this rudeness affects our closest relationships. Pressed for time and unaware of their bad habits, "new rude" couples can spare each other only emotional scraps in their overcommitted and underconnected lives.

Most of this book is meant to be dipped into according to the specific needs you and your partner have. But the lessons in this chapter are elementary and essential for all couples—even if you don't think that rudeness is a problem for you. You will discover simple ways to upgrade your daily communication routine and ward off the creeping influence of the new rudeness. You'll also learn how to use a 5-minute manners conversation that will improve your relationship in a single day.

A "New Rude" Couple

Jim and Laura, both in their thirties, had been married for 7 years when they came to see me. Jim was a vice president at a public relations firm, and Laura was a stay-at-home mom who cared for their two daughters, ages 3 and 5. Jim and Laura's marriage was in serious trouble, and they ended up in my office because they wanted to save it.

They began by telling me about their main problem: They fought about everything. They disagreed about big things like whether Laura should go back to work once their youngest was in nursery school (her husband wanted her to, but she wanted to wait until both kids were in elementary school) and about little things like where to spend the holidays, why Jim often neglected to open his mail, and whether to buy new furniture or stick with what they had. They clashed about the amount of time Jim spent at work in the evenings and how it made Laura feel as though she was a single parent. She begged him to find a new job that would allow him to be home for dinner more often, and he agreed with the idea, but never checked the job listings. Name an issue, and sooner or later Jim and Laura would fight about it. The joyful bubble of their newlywed days had long since burst, and now they both felt lonely and disappointed. The one bright light was that in recent months, they hadn't been fighting as much as they had been before—but on the downside, they concluded that this was because they'd simply given up and were ignoring each other and the issues that led them to fight. The result was that they were spending less time together as a couple and more time with their kids, other family members, and friends. They felt like they had lost the love in their relationship, and they wanted me to help them find it again.

A Telltale Sign

Despite the cracks in their marriage, Jim and Laura appeared calm and collected. When they spoke about their relationship, their indifference to each other was apparent in their choice of words and gestures, which included no visible signs of love or hate. Jim said, "We're just fine, as long as we don't talk about things that really matter." They both admitted that their sex life was nonexistent. As they spoke, their voices sounded monotonous, until I made the following statement.

"I'd like each of you to finish this sentence: 'I want to stay married to my partner because ...' Jim, you first."

Jim hesitated for a moment, then looked straight at me and said, "I want to stay married to Laura because I love her and we have two terrific kids."

Then it was Laura's turn. Without hesitation she said, "I want to stay married to Jim because we have two kids, and I love him too, but the truth is that I don't like him."

Laura's response, "I love him, but I don't like him," was quite revealing. I've heard this mixed message from many of my clients, and what it tells me is that two people are not being kind to one another. We don't like people who don't treat us well, whether we're on the playground or in our living room with our spouse. A couple can love each other because of the label and duties of a marriage, or because they are coparents, or because they remember the glow of courtship, or because underneath it all, they do appreciate each other's character and positive traits. But a repeated lack of kindness would cause anyone to prefer to keep their distance from their partner. Though there are many components to a couple's interaction, I find consistently that disgruntled couples treat each other with very poor manners.

Fight Human Nature: Wake Up or Break Up

Do not decide that someone is good until you see how he or she acts at home.
—THE TALMUD

I am sure that everyone reading this book was raised to have good manners. We were taught that rudeness is unacceptable. And when we first dated our partner, we knew the right things to say and all the right moves to make. We would never dream of not saying hello to our special someone when he or she entered the room. We would politely thank our honey when he or she did something nice for us.

So what happened? Was there a day when we decided that manners were foolish and a waste of our time? No way. It's just that when we get comfortable with someone, human nature leads us to make less of an effort. When we know we can count on our mate to be there no matter what, we don't think we need to be on "good behavior." Unfortunately, when we're no longer trying to incorporate positive, polite behaviors, rudeness creeps in—little things at first, like not saying thank you or skipping a good-night kiss, then bigger and bigger ones, like paying attention to our BlackBerry instead of our partner or talking on the cell phone throughout an entire meal while on a family vacation. Gradually, the negatives loom larger and we can't help but zoom in on them. We pay more and more attention to our unmet expectations until suddenly, without warning, we have entered a rough period of love under fire.

When my husband and I were first married, we were always excited to see each other at the end of the day. When one of us got home from work, we'd stop whatever we were doing to greet one another with a hug. But after only 1 year of marriage, I realized that something had changed. For example, if I was on the phone when my husband walked in the door, I would barely look up before continuing my conversation. I thought, "Why should I rush my phone call when my husband will be around all evening?" It seemed like such a little thing, but the truth was, I could tell that he was stung. With this tiny act of rudeness I was creating a wedge between us. My good habit of lovingly greeting my husband had been replaced by a new, rude habit of indifference. Even when you have the best intentions, a bad habit can cause your relationship to veer off course occasionally. But once I became aware that what I was doing was damaging our relationship, I was able to change my behavior. It's vital to be conscious of your communication routines and how they affect each of you.

Your Communication Routine: A Top Priority

Even if you're on the right track, you'll get run over if you just sit there.

−WILL ROGERS

The only way to keep each other in the spotlight is to consciously choose to have a positive daily communication routine. What's a communication routine? It's the collection of simple habits of interaction that all couples engage in every day. Do you greet each other upon entering and leaving the house? Do you still say good night? Do you compliment each other? Do you say "I love you" in some way each day?

I know from years of mediating couple disputes that when a couple's communication routine is weak, so is their relationship. On the other hand, a high-level communication routine makes you feel bonded and appreciated. As a result, you are more likely to give each other the benefit of the doubt when conflicts arise and obstacles intervene. You have a constant connection that gives you the strength to withstand pressure from outside forces.

TAKE NOTE

The quality of your daily communication routine sets the tone for your entire relationship.

A Snapshot of Jim and Laura's Communication Routine

I asked Jim and Laura to paint a picture of their communication routine.

"Laura and Jim, I want to ask you some brief questions about your day," I said. "Laura, do you usually see Jim in the morning before he leaves for work?"

"Yes," Laura answered. "On most days my alarm goes off at 7:00 a.m., when we both get up."

"Do you say anything to Jim when you get up?" I asked.

"Yes, that's when I usually remind him of the things he has to do that day."

"Do you say good morning or give him a quick peck on the cheek before offering your list of reminders?"

"No," Jim quickly jumped in. "She tells me things while I'm half awake. Then she goes to the bathroom and rushes out to make sure the girls are up."

"All right. Jim, when you get home from work, what do you usually do?"

"I guess I change out of my work clothes and peek in to see what the kids are doing."

Laura chimed in now, "And then what? You go straight to the computer, and I have to pull you away for dinner."

"Well," I said, "I'm getting a good sense of your daily routine, but let me ask you a few more questions. Jim, when was the last time you told Laura that you love her?"

"I don't know," he said.

"I know," Laura answered. "Never. Oh, wait a minute, maybe he did say it to me last Valentine's Day, but getting him to say 'I love you' without it being some major occasion is like pulling teeth! It sure would be nice to hear those words once in a while, considering how much I do for him and the girls."

"Really?" Jim bounced back. "And when was the last time you told me you love me? Do you think I don't want to hear those words?"

"Okay, okay," I cut in to disengage them from their heated exchange. "It seems both of you would like to hear the words 'I love you' more often. But for now let's move on to my last question. Laura, do you think Jim ever does anything worthy of a compliment?"

"Sure, he does," said Laura.

"All right," I said, "then tell me something nice or kind that he did yesterday."

Laura was silent, seeming to rack her brain. "I can't think of anything good from yesterday," she answered.

"Is that so?" Jim instantly challenged her. "What about dinner? I went out of my way after work yesterday to drive to Antonio's to get you that special thin-crust pizza with mushrooms that you love. I didn't have to do that. I did it because I know how much you like it. I think that makes me a pretty good guy. You can't even give me credit for that?"

"No," Laura shrugged. "I do so much for you that getting me pizza is no big deal."

Rudeness, Interrupted

It became quite clear to me that Laura and Jim had established a very weak communication routine. They didn't say good morning, thank you, hello, good-bye, or "I love you" on a regular basis. Each opportunity for a warm moment of connection was dismissed. Their communication habits displayed mutual neglect and misplaced priorities. They took each other for granted, and each of them had adopted a defensive attitude: "Why should I compliment you when no one compliments me? Why should I say 'I love you' when I don't hear those words myself? Why should I thank you for going out of your way for me when you don't thank me for the countless things I do for you each day?" Many unhappy couples get caught up in this sad, petty thought process that they feel protects their vulnerability. If that's your mentality, I want you to get rid of it now. In order to break out of your rudeness deadlock, one of you has to become a great partner and decide to make the first move in the right direction. Are you going to be the one?

If you're wondering what's so important about saying good morning or good night, consider this: My company conducted an online survey of people in committed relationships. We asked participants if their mate had said good morning, good night, and/or "I love you" on the previous day. Eighty-two percent of people who rated their relationship as excellent or very good had heard *all three*. In contrast, of the people who rated their relationship as poor or below average, more than half hadn't heard any one of those comments!

Whether poor manners lead to a weak relationship or vice versa, it's clear that a couple's daily communication routine is intimately linked to overall relationship happiness. Simple comments that take only seconds a day to express form the foundation of a strong communication routine. No matter what the state of your current communication routine is, let's take a look at some new verbal habits that will bring positive change to your relationship.

The Five Vital Habits: Installing a High-Level Communication Routine

To instantly upgrade your communication routine, make these five crucial habits a nonnegotiable part of your daily repertoire. The goal here is to use the five vitals *consistently*—and yes, that means every single day, unless your schedule prevents it—to let your mate know that your relationship is your number one priority. Once you get the hang of these five habits, you may want to add other good-manners habits that work for you as a couple.

1. Greetings: "Hello" and "Good-Bye"

Do you habitually say hello or good-bye to your mate as one of you enters or exits the home? It is the least you can do to acknowledge that your mate's presence means something to you. A simple hello says, "I'm happy to see you. I'm here for you." A sincere good-bye says, "I know you're going out into the world now, and I care that you are leaving. I'll miss you." When you tell your mom that you'll call her back because your husband just got home or you put the newspaper down to say hello, you are being kind, responsive, and well-mannered. You are making your mate your top priority.

Whether it's you or your mate who is coming or going, I challenge you to be the first one to offer a greeting today. Don't say, "Why should I say it? He could just as easily say it first." Keep in mind that if you have a race to the bottom, you will end up at the bottom. By taking a little initiative, you will end up at the top.

2. "Good Morning"

TAKE NOTE

Our survey showed that 94 percent of people who hear the magic words "good morning" every day said that their relationship was very good to excellent.

At first, even I was shocked by that statistic. I knew there was a strong connection between good manners and a good relationship, but 94 percent? But then I thought about what "good morning" really means, and the figure started to make a lot more sense. When I say good morning to my husband, what I really mean is "It is a good morning because I am alive and you are here with me.

It is a good morning because we're healthy, or if one of us is sick, then it's a good morning because we can help and support each other." There are spiritual meanings that come through the two simple words "good morning." Each of us can uncover our own meanings for those words. What does "good morning" mean to you? And what do you have to lose by sharing it with your mate?

3. "Good Night"

Do you make it a habit to end your day with the loving words "good night"? You may think, "What's the big deal about saying that?" Well, folks, it's a very big deal. We don't always go to bed at the same time as our partner. So without a "good night," someone is left alone, possibly watching television, finishing up some work, or reading a book, completely unaware of whether or not his or her partner is awake. This is a rude, cold, and isolating habit. When you don't bother to say "good night," you give the impression that you couldn't care less about your partner or the relationship. What a shame, since one of the nicest parts of living with a partner is being part of one another's lives in every way. I don't mean you have to alert your partner every time you open the fridge or take a shower, but ending your day and going to sleep is actually relevant to the mate who shares your life and your bed. Establish a meaningful nighttime ritual as your final loving connection of the day—even if it's just a quick kiss accompanied by the words "good night."

4. "I Love You for [Fill in the Blank]."

One morning as I prepared to brush my teeth, I looked down at the bathroom sink and found a pleasant surprise. I'd expected to see the rolled-up, squeezed-out tube of toothpaste that I had left lying there the night before, when I had been too lazy to walk down the hall to get a new one. Instead, there was a brand-new tube, unused and still sealed. My husband had finished the old toothpaste after me and replaced it so I would have a fresh tube in the morning. When I finished brushing my teeth, I told my husband how much I appreciated this small gesture. "I love you for leaving a new tube of toothpaste in the bathroom for me. It was really nice of you." When I was single, I probably wouldn't have thought anything about a small toothpaste deed. But after being married and realizing that keeping love alive is a daily choice, I know that forgetting to express my appreciation for such acts of kindness is tantamount to forgetting to tell my husband that I love him.

For most of us, it's all too easy to see the handful of irritating things our partner does, but it's much harder to take notice of the many kind, generous, compassionate, supportive deeds he or she does every day. It's time to adjust your radar screen to pick up on the many small things that make you love your mate—and let him know!

5. A Compliment

You might feel like this is a moot point. After all, how many times can you tell your wife that she looks beautiful or that you love her? How often can you compliment your husband's choice of sweaters? The answer is: as often as you can, as long as your words are sincere. But just as important, on the days when something visible (such as a new haircut or tie) doesn't capture your attention, find another way to offer a compliment. For example, "You are so kind to take your mother to the doctor." Or, "You are such a devoted father. You have so much patience with the kids." Or, "It was really thoughtful of you to call your friend to see how his job interview went." People in healthy relationships know that it's important to compliment good character traits in their mate, while people in poor relationships tend to skip over them.

> ## HAVE YOU HEARD?
> When we asked people whether they would prefer to be compli-mented for being kind or good-looking, 84 percent said they'd rather be praised for being kind.

Change your focus today. Be on the lookout for the visible and nonvisible attributes that make your partner special and unique. You can discern nonvisible reasons for compliments by asking yourself: Is my partner generous, compassionate, kind, or caring to me or to our children, parents, friends, neighbors, or family? The best part of this is that the more you value your partner, the more your partner will value you. The shortest distance between two people is a compliment.

The 5-Minute Manners Conversation

Now that you understand how simple it is to incorporate the five vital habits into your everyday life, it's time to implore your mate to join you.

Step #1: State of Affairs

Say to your partner, "I've noticed that we barely say good morning and good night to each other, or hello and good-bye, and that we rarely compliment each other or say 'I love you.'"

Step #2: Ask for What You Want

"I want to improve my manners. I want you to know how much I admire and love you every day. You deserve it. Will you try to do this for me too? It'll only take us a few seconds a day to be kinder to each other."

Step #3: Speak of the Future

"If one of us starts letting our manners slide, let's agree to tell each other. It seems so easy to make this small change in our words, and it can only make our relationship better, don't you think?"

Throw Out the Scorecard

Even after you have a 5-minute manners conversation, it may take a little while for your partner to get the hang of this new habit. Don't let that keep you from following through on your end of the deal. I know you want a better relationship, and I applaud you for looking for ways to make it work rather than an excuse to let it end. The one stumbling block that will defeat every effort for improvement is to stubbornly carry the thought that your partner must respond to every one of your initiatives, turn by turn. This is not a chess game. You may have to make 10 moves in a row before your partner makes one. Concentrate on your goal and on what you are saying and doing to achieve it, not on what your mate isn't doing.

If you are consistent with your good manners but your mate neglects his or hers and a week goes by and you are getting edgy, address the issue again. Remind your mate that you need him or her to do this because it's the first step to a better relationship. Be sure your partner understands that you are serious about this and that you interpret positive manners—or the lack of them—as a reflection of his love for you.

SHORT-CIRCUIT AN ARGUMENT: STOP THE LION THAT ROARS

There are two sides to every argument, until you take one.

—MILTON BERLE

WHETHER THEY KNOW it or not, every couple gets into dumb arguments. You and your mate have probably butted heads over trivial details like the name of an Italian restaurant where you had dinner 2 years ago, the date of a friend's birthday, or the cost of a new flat-screen TV. Or you've found yourself bickering over whose turn it is to do the dishes or pick up milk. At their worst, disagreements like these jump-start a battle royal between you and your honey, and you find yourself in a shouting match over something that's insignificant in the big picture of your lives together. An evening of companionship is ruined by a few of the wrong words spoken at the wrong time.

These arguments may not seem like a big deal, but they create tiny cracks in your relationship. They are holes through which energy, joy, and goodwill seep out, little by little, day by day. The good news is that you can plug those holes. All it takes to stop one of these energy-sucking spats is a little wisdom.

Are You Conflict Wise?

Wisdom is the ability to observe what's happening while it's happening, to step back and use prior experience to figure out where the situation is headed, and then to select a better, alternate route. Being conflict wise means knowing that the words you are about to say may kick off a fight and then choosing a different approach so you and your partner avoid that fight and arrive at a peaceful resolution. We tend to think that some people are just born with this kind of wisdom. But anyone can acquire the skills to wisely avoid conflict. George Bernard Shaw said, "We are made wise not by the recollection of our past, but by the responsibility for our future." When you are conflict wise, you vigilantly look out for the minefields that arouse dumb arguments and sidestep them so you arrive at a better future.

This chapter sheds new light on common conversations that often lead to all-out arguments. The goal is for you to become wise about your approach and learn how to short-circuit these ticking time bombs in three ways: by becoming aware of the top five types of dumb arguments; by learning how to pick only the right battles; and finally, by being able to power down your aggression and power up your relationship with a 5-minute conversation that helps you extinguish needless conflict.

The Top Five Dumb Arguments

If you've ever watched the show *Everybody Loves Raymond,* you know how quickly a couple can get into an explosive argument over nothing. Well, it's not just Ray and Debra who have dumb fights. We all do. In fact, even the smartest people have dumb fights. Here are examples of the five most common types of dumb arguments that my clients have with their partners.

1. The Dumb Premature Argument

Hector and Maria live in an apartment but hope to buy a house someday. Every time they visit a friend who lives in a house, their drive home provides ample time for squabbling about whether they should buy a ranch-style home like the one Maria grew up in or a two-story colonial like the one Hector's family had. They argue vehemently about the pros and cons of each style, but the silly thing is, they aren't planning to move out of their apartment until their toddler is ready for kindergarten, at least 3 years from now. Even if they managed to argue their way to a decision now, in all likelihood they would have to reargue the same issue in 3 years anyway, because their preferences, incomes, and family situation would likely change over time.

The Wise Tactic

If the outcome of any argument can't be acted upon for a long time, it's a dumb premature argument. As much as you might *want* to voice your side now, you'll only be wasting time and energy—and adding unnecessary conflict to your relationship. When you realize that you're arguing about something that doesn't need an immediate decision, it's wise to short-circuit the fight by saying, "Why don't we wait to have this discussion until we actually need to?" In the case of Hector and Maria, one of them simply needs to say, "Why are we wasting our time arguing about this now? Let's make a pact not to debate our design preferences until we're actually ready to buy a house!" This will give your partner the ability to retreat gracefully with a comment like "That's a good idea. I don't know why we started talking about this now anyway."

2. The Dumb "Whatever" Argument

As Elissa is occupied with getting her kids ready for bed, her husband, Jason, makes a suggestion: "Why don't I get tickets for a play on Saturday night in 3 weeks? We don't have plans for that night."

"Sure," Elissa says, half-listening. "That sounds great."

"Is there any show you especially want to see?" Jason asks. Elissa can't think of one at that moment because she's focused on getting her son into his pajamas. She says, "Whatever you want is fine."

The next day her husband tells her he got tickets to *Take It or Leave It,* a comedy about couples. "I can't believe you bought tickets for that lousy show," she groans. "It got terrible reviews. Don't you remember that I told you my friend Rachel and her husband walked out during the intermission?"

"No, you never told me that!" Jason shoots back. "Besides, you said I should get tickets to whatever show I wanted, so I did."

"Yeah, but I didn't think you'd pick *that* show," Elissa snaps. "It's a waste of our money."

The Wise Tactic

"Whatever" is a dangerous word. When you use it in response to a question of choice, you automatically give up your right to complain about the outcome. Save the use of "whatever" for only those situations in which you truly don't care about the decision. Never use it when you're too busy or lazy to think through what you want. Just ask for more time. Elissa could have simply said, "Honey, can you give me a minute? Once I get the kids into bed we can go online and see which shows look the best." Asking for more time may seem like a pain at that moment, but it's worth it if it will help you enjoy the outcome and avoid an argument.

3. The Dumb Director Argument

Alex and Beth are doing some redecorating in their home. Alex walks into a room where Beth has recently hung two pictures. He notices that they are not hanging at the same height, so he calls out to Beth, who is seated in the next room. "Hey, come here," he says. "You hung this picture too low. You need to fix it."

To Alex's dismay, Beth doesn't budge. She shouts back, "It's fine the way it is. Don't be such a perfectionist."

"Maybe you shouldn't do a job if you can't do it right!" he yells. Not the nicest way to begin a Sunday afternoon together.

Alex gave Beth a director's order. He saw a problem and knew exactly how to fix it, so he came right out and told her what to do. Unfortunately, no one responds well to being bossed around. Issuing orders is probably the worst way to try to get your partner to do something, and it will likely result in a dumb argument.

The Wise Tactic

Instead of giving a director's order when you want something done, use this quick two-step approach: (1) Make a statement about the situation, and (2) ask the leading question "What do you think?" Your goal here is to start a conversation in which the person becomes aware of the problem and makes an independent decision to do something about it. For example, Alex could have said, "Beth, I think the pictures aren't quite lining up. What do you think?" Saying this would have piqued Beth's curiosity and motivated her to come back into the room. At that point she probably would have seen the problem for herself and decided to fix it. In just minutes Alex could have gotten what he wanted *and* avoided a dumb argument.

4. The Dumb Post-Argument Argument

Natalie and Sean decide to take their two kids, ages 5 and 8, on a weekend visit to Sean's parents. It's about a 3-hour trip by car or train. Natalie desperately wants to drive, while Sean wants to take the train.

"It's so much easier to take the car," explains Natalie. "We have all of the kids' stuff, and we can throw it in the trunk. Besides, the kids can sleep in the car on the way home. And we won't have to wait for a taxi at the train station."

"But what about me? I'll be tired too," declares Sean. "If we take the train, I can read and rest."

"But it'll be late when we get home, and the kids have to go to school on Monday," says Natalie. "They need to be able to sleep in the car. They'll just run around on the train."

"Yeah, but I have to go to work on Monday, and I'd like to get some rest on the train," Sean retorts.

Like a ping-pong match, the "yeah, buts" are volleyed back and forth as Natalie's and Sean's voices get louder. Finally Sean shouts, "All right, all right, I'll drive the stupid car."

"Great," says Natalie, who should say thank you because she got what she wanted. But she doesn't. Instead, she continues to go on about why it's so much better for them to drive than to take the train. The more she talks, the more irritated Sean gets and the less Sean wants to drive. In fact, he is almost at the point of demanding that they cancel the trip and saying they should all stay home.

The Wise Tactic

When you get what you want, stop talking. The argument is over when you both agree on an outcome. Don't press the issue simply because you want the other person to agree with your reasoning, too. As the expression goes, "Quit while you're ahead!"

5. The Dumb Factual Argument

My husband and I were driving to a 99¢ store to buy some party supplies. I mentioned, "You know, a lot of these so-called 99¢ stores charge more than 99¢ for many of the items they sell."

"Not possible," he said. "All 99¢ stores sell everything at that price. That's why they're called 99¢ stores."

"That's not true. You don't know because you haven't been to one. The 99¢ thing is just a way to get more people into the store," I explained.

"Why would they call it a 99¢ store if it's not one?" he shot back, still trying to convince me.

"Wait a minute," I blurted out. "This is a dumb argument. We're arguing about a fact. Why don't we just hold on for 10 minutes, get to the store, and we'll have our answer?" He agreed, so we shut our mouths and found the answer in the store. (I was right!)

The following week, I was explaining this dumb argument theory to my aunt and she realized that she had just fallen victim to this type of fight herself. "Last Friday night," she told me, "your uncle and I were talking about old times and the fabulous first apartment we had in New York City on East 75th Street. As soon as I mentioned the apartment address, your uncle, Mr. Know-It-All, disagreed. Then I said, 'No, you're wrong,' and he swore up and down that he was right. I told him that he had a lousy memory. Of course he yelled at me for that one! It turned into a big argument."

My aunt could have ended that rift before it began if she had been conflict wise. Rather than continuing on the path to conflict, she should have said, "We're having a dumb argument. Let's just look up the answer."

The Wise Tactic

Have you ever found yourself getting agitated because your partner says you're wrong when you're sure you're right? Or have you found yourself trading "It's true" and "No, it isn't" until you're both blue in the face? Those are all familiar set-up words for the dumb factual argument. Instead, when you are bickering about a fact like an address, a name, or a statistic, recognize this and say, "Hey, we're arguing about a fact. Let's just find out the information instead of fighting about it." With the help of Google, you'll have your answer and avoid an argument over nothing.

The 5-Minute Conversation: Short-Circuit a Dumb Argument

> *It's so simple to be wise. Just think of something stupid and don't say it.*
> —SAM LEVENSON

Despite your best intentions, you may still find yourself getting tangled up in stupid spats. No matter who started the fight, you can use your new wisdom to stop it. When you see that you and your mate are headed down the road to a dumb argument, here's how to short-circuit it.

1. Admit Your Error

Switch gears as soon as you realize you shouldn't have picked this battle because the issue is trivial, or you're arguing about a fact, or you gave an order, or you said "whatever," or you're having a "post-argument" or a premature argument. Hold up your hands as if to surrender and admit your error with a simple comment that identifies why you're having a dumb argument. For example, you could say, "Wait a second. I shouldn't have said that. This is silly because we are having a dumb argument about something that's a fact."

2. No Buts About It

If your mate doesn't want to short-circuit the argument and tries to continue with a comment like "But just let me explain," let him or her talk, and then short-circuit the potential argument again by saying, "Well, that could be, but there's no point in debating it." Just keep up that response and your partner will eventually have to let it go.

Pick the Right Battles

We've all heard the saying "You have to pick your battles." That sounds good, but what does it mean when it comes to love? How do we know which battles to pick and which ones to skip? Is there a way to decide what really matters?

You already know how to identify and avoid the five most common dumb arguments. But there are plenty of other scenarios that can launch pointless clashes—typically, when your mate does something that irritates or inconveniences you. He or she doesn't seem to think it's a problem, but you do. When that happens, use the following two-step "pick your battle" process to help you decide whether to let your feelings be known or to zip your lips.

1. Inspect

Look past the person who caused the problem and instead look at the situation, like it or not. Ask yourself, "Is it possible to change or fix the situation right now, or is it too late?"

2. Accept or Reject

If it's too late to change the situation and nobody is harmed, then bite your tongue and accept it. But if it can be changed without causing a major disturbance, you should speak up once you have a viable solution in mind.

Repeat Offenders

If the problem happens repeatedly, be assertive and explain that you need to come up with a specific prevention plan together. For instance, if your dog often has accidents in the house because of a miscommunication about who was supposed to take him for a walk, then prevent the problem from happening again by coming up with a solution, such as creating a dog walking schedule.

Should Jen Pick This Battle?

Jen and Mike arrive at a popular restaurant they've been meaning to check out for a while. Jen tells the maître d' that they have a reservation under their last name, Singer. When the maître d' says, "I don't see that name on the list; could it be under another name?" Mike looks to Jen and asks, "What name did you use?"

"Me? Didn't you make the reservation?" Jen responds.

"No, I didn't. You said you were going to."

The maître d' sees a problem coming, so he quickly chimes in, "That's all right. We're fully booked, but if you can wait 15 minutes, I'll be able to seat you in the bar area, which has the same menu."

"Okay," Jen reluctantly says as they silently walk to the less romantic bar area. Jen clearly remembers when and where Mike said he would call for the reservation. The dilemma now is, should she sit down, order a glass of wine, and try to forget about the mistake (which, thankfully, doesn't happen often)? Or should she lay out the evidence to prove that he, not she, messed up their dinner?

By using the pick-your-battle process, Jen will conclude that she should *not* pick this battle.

1. Inspect

They are already at the restaurant, and she cannot go back in time to fix the reservation oversight.

2. Accept or Reject

Jen should accept the situation because it is after the fact. Nothing can be done to fix it now. Although it's not her preference, they will be seated in the bar area in 15 minutes. There would be no point in going to another restaurant where they also wouldn't have a reservation. And since this mistake doesn't happen often, Mike is not a repeat offender, so there is no need to come up with a plan of prevention for the future.

There is no doubt that it would be hard for Jen to just let the battle go, because she believes that she has a chain of evidence to prove that she is right that her husband was supposed to make the reservation. But since this oversight doesn't happen often, she should chalk it up to a miscommunication. As disappointed as she may be, arguing will only make the situation worse. If Jen can move past her urge to fight about it, they might still be able to have the enjoyable dinner she had hoped for.

Be a Wise Couple

It can be hard to give up the habit of getting into dumb arguments. No one likes conflict, but most of us do like to be right. So we plunge into silly disagreements, trying to prove that we know best, trying to get our way, trying to *win*.

Here's a very old piece of relationship advice: You can be right, or you can be happy. Now that you've read this chapter, you have the awareness and knowledge to steer clear of useless battles and build a stronger partnership. Instead of insisting on always being right, you can wisely choose to have a more loving relationship. Apply your new skills, and in 5 minutes or less you'll be a happier couple.

5

INSPIRE APPRECIATION: END RELATIONSHIP MADNESS

A woman is standing nude, looking in the bedroom mirror. She is not happy with what she sees and says to her husband, "I feel horrible; I look old, fat, and ugly. I really need you to pay me a compliment."

The husband replies, "Your eyesight's near perfect."

—ANONYMOUS

REMEMBER THAT EXCITING day when you realized you wanted to commit to being a permanent fixture in your partner's life? Well, whether you realized it or not, on that very same day you made another commitment—to cherish your mate by being his or her head cheerleader. This is one of the most important roles for a loving mate, but its importance is often underestimated. While most jobs can be done by any number of people, if you allow the job of being a loving, caring, appreciative cheerleader for your

partner to fall to someone else, your relationship will most definitely suffer.

Unfortunately, many of us either just don't take this job seriously, or relinquish it early on in a relationship by going on auto-
pilot and taking things for granted. You may think, "Of course she
knows I appreciate her—I married her, didn't I?" This assumption conveniently lets us off the hook from doing and saying the
things that show we care. Couples tend to develop five types of
relationship madness, each one a negative thought process that
kills off appreciation. We will discuss how to identify and overcome each type of madness later in the chapter.

Sometimes a lack of appreciation in a relationship comes from
a desire for revenge. For a handful of my clients, the denial of
appreciation is not simply a bad habit of neglect that innocently
grew over time, but rather an attempt to punish one's mate for not
doing what is wanted or expected. The punisher makes excuses
for not giving appreciation by thinking things like "I'm not going
to tell her I appreciate some of the things she does for me unless
she stops telling her mother about everything she thinks I do
wrong." Or, "I work so hard taking care of our kids, but I never get
any credit for it. Why should I have to appreciate someone who
doesn't give *me* any credit?" Denying appreciation is one way a
partner can feel like he or she can affect or punish the mate.

I want you to separate your partner's mistakes and wrongdo-
ings from the positive and helpful things he or she does. Realize
that when you show appreciation, you are not pretending that
your mate is perfect, nor are you accepting his or her wrongdo-
ings. You can and should address each of your mate's missteps by
using the appropriate 5-minute conversations in this book. With
an effective method for dealing with your mate's imperfections,
you can then refocus your attention on your mate's perfections.

TAKE NOTE

Cherishing your mate means identifying and appreciating your partner's positive behaviors and actions.

It's time for you to point out the positive behaviors and actions that you would like to see happen more often. What is appreciated is reinforced. Sometimes it's our partner who has abandoned his or her cheerleading responsibilities. Sometimes it's you. Maybe both of you have simultaneously relinquished that role. It doesn't matter how it started—it's time for both of you to reclaim this valuable role.

The Three Zones of Relationships

Couples live in one of three different relationship zones. As newly dating couples, we all start out in an "ideal zone." In this zone, giddy with infatuation, we recognize and appreciate the good things about our mate and ignore the bad. If a friend says something uncomplimentary about our mate, we quickly stand up for him or her.

As time passes, most of us move into the "real zone," where we recognize both the positive and negative qualities of our mate. This is a healthy zone to live in. If a couple remains in this zone, their relationship can survive and thrive.

Then there are those couples who slide into the third zone, the "danger zone." In this zone the relationship takes on a darker cast. Both partners feel distant, unappreciated, and undervalued. They question their commitment to each other. They contemplate ending the relationship or separating. Some of these couples have fallen victim to gender roles that define responsibilities so strictly that tasks become obligations undeserving of appreciation. Others express only words of ingratitude and dissatisfaction to their partners.

All of these danger-zone couples are stuck in a conflict-filled rut. They can't see their partner's good traits (and I know they are there, because when anyone starts a relationship, it's because he or she loves and likes the person), and they focus only on the flaws, which under the lens of such constant scrutiny have taken on an even greater appearance.

Some people instantly know that their relationship is suffering from a serious appreciation deficit and is creeping toward or existing in the danger zone, while others are less certain. Take this simple test to find out which zone you occupy.

Relationship Zone Test: What's Your Appreciation Number?

For the next 2 days, follow your usual schedule of activities, but:

1. Count the number of times you say thank you to your mate.
2. Count the number of times your mate says thank you to you.

Scoring

Use the thank-you number that is lower, either yours or your mate's, to determine your relationship zone. For example, if you said thank you seven times over the 2-day period and your mate said it only once, then 1 is your score for this test.

6 or More: The Ideal Zone

You are living in the ideal zone. That's quite impressive considering that you are in a committed relationship and no longer just dating. It's clear that both of you recognize that random acts of kindness are worthy of appreciation. Keep it up!

2 to 5: *The Real Zone*

You are living in the real zone. You and your mate may not gush over each other all the time, but you do meaningfully thank each other for the kind and helpful things you do for each other. These verbal expressions create much of the glue that bonds the two of you together. You're doing well, but beware: If you begin to take your mate for granted, you can easily plunge into the danger zone (especially if you scored toward the lower end of this range). Research shows that most relationships worsen over time, and yours will too, unless you make a conscious effort to sustain positive appreciation habits.

Less than 2: *The Danger Zone*

Your relationship is in the danger zone, and it is suffering from a serious appreciation deficit. You must focus on this problem immediately or it will fester and cause deeper resentment and relationship destruction. You may be thinking, "I'm in the danger zone because there is nothing for me to express gratitude about. What should I do, make something up?" You shouldn't make something up, but you do need to look deeper. You must uncover some positive things about your mate. You may have become blind to the good things because you are so focused on the bad things. There is always something to appreciate. So take off your blindfold and pay close attention to the following relationship madness tips and 5-minute conversation.

TAKE NOTE

What is relationship madness? It's when our partner's strengths and assets fade into the background while his or her flaws and liabilities take center stage.

Relationship Madness

A question for you: Do you say thank you to a person who holds a door open for you?

Your answer is probably yes. You specifically notice when a stranger holds the door open for you because that kind of politeness doesn't happen all the time.

But what happens when your mate holds the door open for you? If he or she rarely does it, you probably notice and say thank you. But if your mate always opens the door for you, you come to expect it, and so you stop noticing it and saying thank you.

We thank people for doing things that are out of the ordinary, yet we often fail to praise an act that, even if extraordinary, has become ordinary to us.

It is this type of illogical habit that leads us to eventually ignore what is good in our mate and focus on what is wrong. We must be alert to this tendency and use reason and logic to combat it.

There are five types of relationship madness that prevent us from noticing and commenting on what is good and worthy in our partner. Each type is a stumbling block we must remove with logical thinking. If any of the following types of madness sound familiar to you, you owe it to your relationship, to use the corresponding appreciation tip to fix it. Giving more appreciation will inspire your mate to respond in kind.

Relationship Madness Type #1: "I don't have to thank her for something she benefited from."

"Why should I thank her for buying the lawn chairs for the backyard? She sits on them too."

"Why should I thank him for throwing out the garbage? It stinks and I know he doesn't want to smell it any more than I do."

Do you recognize yourself or your partner in any of these statements? It's not surprising because this "Well, you benefited too!" attitude is the most dominant type of relationship madness I encounter among my clients. Holding on to this mind-set is absurd because it means that any time your partner does something that benefits you, it doesn't deserve a thank-you unless your partner did *not* benefit from it in any way. Talk about a win-lose attitude.

Thank-yous should be given when your partner does things just for you *and also* when he or she does things for "us" the couple, the household, or the family. If you're not convinced that you want to thank your mate for doing something that benefits the two of you, then just add two powerful words to the end of the sentence: "Thank you for getting milk *for us*." You'll see that your mate is more than happy to receive that kind of thank-you. Remember that no matter how easy or expected it was, you didn't put in the time or energy to do it, your partner did, so let him or her know that you appreciate it.

TAKE NOTE

Your partner may have benefited from his or her good deed, but so did you. That's always worthy of a thank-you.

Relationship Madness Type #2: "He didn't do it right, so why should I thank him?"

Relationship madness struck me one rainy night after I called my husband to ask him to stop at the drugstore to pick up diapers for our son on his way home from work. I specifically told him the size, brand, and type I wanted. "No problem," he said. "I'll be home in about an hour." He came home with the right size and brand, but the wrong type. My first thought was "He didn't listen to me! This is so annoying. I should have gone to the store myself."

I was mad and tired after working and taking care of my son. I definitely was in no mood to thank my husband for bringing home the wrong diapers. But as I stared at the diaper package sitting neatly on the table, a rational thought hit me. Although my husband didn't get exactly what I told him to get, I remembered that he also worked hard and he went out of his way to stop at the drugstore to buy the diapers, which were definitely usable, just not exactly what I wanted. And he did save me a trip to the drugstore. Maybe he did deserve a thank-you.

This is a quintessential moment in a relationship, one when logic must overcome emotion. It is madness to criticize someone who makes an effort, even if that effort doesn't result in your perfect outcome (like when your partner buys whole milk when you wanted 2 percent). If we judge people this way, especially mates, we will never have a good relationship, and in general, our mate will not agree to do anything for us for fear of making a mistake.

With that idea in mind, I said, "Thanks for getting the diapers and saving me a trip to the drugstore. Next time, please get the other type—they fit him better—but these will still work." I didn't ignore the mistake; I just made it less important than his helpfulness. The next time he went to buy diapers, I wrote down the specifics for him!

TAKE NOTE

If you criticize someone for trying, they won't want to try again. Don't let what is wrong cancel out the appreciation for what is right.

Relationship Madness Type #3: "He only did it because I told him to."

Lisa and Jeff met with me in mediation to work out problems they were having with sharing child care responsibilities for their two children. Their story perfectly exemplifies the third common type of relationship madness that most of us suffer from at some time.

Lisa wanted Jeff to take more responsibility for the kids on weekends so she could have some free time for herself. She asked him to take their two boys to a nearby park for a few hours. Jeff agreed and packed a bag with drinks and a softball. When they got back from the park a few hours later, all of them were quite tired and needed some downtime.

I asked Lisa what she said to Jeff when he returned. "I asked if they had a good time," she said.

"Why didn't you thank him for taking the kids to the park?" I asked. Her answer? "Why would I thank him? He only took them to the park because I told him to. He should have known I was tired and offered to take the kids to the park without me telling him to do it."

"Yes," I responded to Lisa, "he could have offered. But he did go to the park with the kids, and you did get the free time you wanted. He could have said no." Lisa was so caught up with what her partner *didn't* do (offer to take the kids) that she didn't think to show any appreciation for what he *did* do (take the kids to the park). Lisa needed to understand that asking her mate to do something for her didn't make his actions any less valuable or worthy of her appreciation than if he had done the same thing without being asked.

Relationship Madness Type #4: "I expect her to do that. I don't have to say thank you."

We often overlook the positive and helpful things our partner does consistently and frequently, such as taking out the garbage, going to the supermarket, working long hours to support the family, and helping the kids with their homework. We take those things for granted, and it's easy for them to fade into the background and go unnoticed. Instead, we notice the less common negative things that disturb our pattern. Human nature encourages us to focus our attention not on the background noise, but on the loud, imminent siren.

Consider this: I once had a boss at a law firm who was disliked by his employees because they felt he never showed any appreciation for their efforts. One day he told me that he'd fired his gardeners because they kept breaking his sprinkler heads by rolling the lawn mowers over them. He had hired new gardeners and was very happy with them because they were keeping his lawn and sprinklers in tip-top shape.

"Did you say anything to your new gardeners?" I asked my boss. "What do you mean?" he replied.

"Well, I thought you might have thanked them for doing such a good job, especially since you fired your previous gardeners for doing such a terrible job."

"Thank them? You must be kidding. Why would I do that? I pay them well, so I expect them to do a good job."

So there it was: his attitude of ingratitude. It was the same attitude he expressed toward his staff, and it was suddenly clear why people didn't like him or working for him. He expected that if you were getting compensated for a job financially, you didn't also need a verbal pat on the back. He was terribly stingy with his words of appreciation.

When your mate does ordinary—but nice—things, do you praise and appreciate him or her for meeting your expectations? Or because he or she is your mate, do you simply expect her to provide a certain level of support? Just because you expect your partner to do certain things doesn't make those acts any less worthy of appreciation. If they benefit you in any way, they deserve to be recognized.

TAKE NOTE
When your mate's actions meet any of your expectations, verbally recognize his or her effort by saying: "Thank you for _____."

Relationship Madness Type #5: "I don't have to be appreciative when my partner does something nice for someone other than me."

In your role as head cheerleader, it is your responsibility to be aware of and comment on the times when your partner displays compassion, generosity, or kindness to anyone—whether that's you, a friend, a relative, or a perfect stranger. For example, if your partner goes on short notice to meet a friend in need who just suffered a bad breakup, it's your job to appreciate him for being a supportive friend. If your husband takes the time to help your son with his science project, it's your job to point out what a great dad he is. If you take the time to help a cousin with a problem, it is up to your mate to recognize and comment on your thoughtfulness even though it has no direct connection to him.

Your partner's friend, your son, and your cousin might also show their appreciation. But you, rather than any of those people, have the sole responsibility of being your mate's head cheerleader. Even if your partner doesn't hear "thank you" from anyone else, he needs to hear it from you.

TAKE NOTE
The best cheerleaders praise their mates for good behavior no matter who benefits from his or her actions.

The 5-Minute Conversation to Change Your Attitude about Gratitude

1. Define the Problem

When you're ready to share what you've learned about relationship madness, tell your mate that you want to have a 5-minute conversation (by telling him or her that it'll only take 5 minutes, you'll get your mate more interested in the conversation).

Then say, "I know that we both care about each other, but I don't think we show each other enough appreciation. It's as if we're so focused on picking out the negative things we say and do that we don't recognize or appreciate the many positive things we do for each other and other people. I want to change this."

Note that including yourself in the problem makes it less likely that your partner will feel as if he or she is being attacked.

2. Offer a Solution

Explain the new information you just learned in this chapter.

For example, you might say, "I think there are lots of things we could appreciate about each other that we often overlook. I know that I have a bad habit of not thanking you for many of the nice things you do, like making dinner, paying the bills, or reading to the kids before bed. I'm going to concentrate on making sure you know how much I appreciate those things."

If more than one type of relationship madness hits home with you, then talk about that too. Once you've explained that you're going to be more aware of the many opportunities to show gratitude, be assertive and ask your mate to also find opportunities to appreciate you.

3. Get Results

If your mate is resistant to your request for more gratitude, it could be because of skepticism that is founded on the debilitating attitude that says "I'm not going to appreciate you until you appreciate me." If this attitude rings true for your mate, I suggest you move past it by honestly following through on your commitment. If your partner is still hesitant about agreeing to change some habits, then proceed on your own to spark a ripple effect or take the assertive approach described below.

The Ripple Effect

The best way to encourage an appreciative attitude is to start a ripple effect. You do this by modeling the behavior you would like to see in your mate. Start handing out those thank yous like they're free. Oh, wait, they *are* free! Before long your mate will enjoy your abundant appreciation and be motivated to reciprocate with smiles and kind words for you.

The Assertive Approach

When you do something worthy of gratitude and don't get it, ask for it. Let's say you and your partner are watching TV and you get up to fetch a snack—and while you're at it, you bring one for him, too. When you offer it to him, he barely looks away from the screen as he grabs and devours it without issuing a word of thanks. In this case, you need to use the assertive approach. Let him know that a little appreciation would have been nice. You might say, "Hey, I know you're focused on watching this show right now, but it would still be nice to know you appreciated the snack. 'Thank you for the snack' would go a long way. I know it's a little thing, but it would really make me happy." Beware that this approach works only if you're generous with appreciation as well.

The Icing on the Cake: Public Appreciation

If you really want to champion your mate and improve your relationship in seconds, show your mate a little public appreciation. Imagine yourself sitting at dinner with another couple when your mate leans over and tells them, "My wife has such a big heart. She spent last Sunday baking dozens of cookies for a bake-sale fund-raiser." Wouldn't a comment like that make you feel loved, cherished, and appreciated? Look for opportunities to create that same feeling for your partner. When you recognize and appreciate your mate publicly, I assure you that your relationship will immediately benefit.

Public appreciation in no way eliminates the need for private compliments. Those should be given on a daily basis, as we saw in Chapter 3 (Tame Rudeness: Install a Daily Communication Routine). But there's something very moving about hearing your partner praise you in public. It says that your partner thinks so highly of you that he or she wants everyone to know how great you are—and what could be better than that? I urge you to go out of your way to find opportunities to appreciate your mate in front of his or her friends and family. In just a single minute you will persuade your mate to like and appreciate you more.

Ode to Imperfection

In a healthy relationship, most of us live in the real zone. We recognize our partner's flaws and deal with them through effective communication, but we also take the time to recognize and admire his or her strengths and attributes. We accept the truth that nobody qualifies as perfect, and we don't let that truth stop us from cheering for the good qualities in our partner—generosity, compassion, kindness, patience.

If it feels overwhelming to you to move your relationship from the danger zone into the real zone, remember that every journey begins with a single step. One kind word, one thank-you, one moment of public appreciation will jump-start the cycle of love and respect you deserve.

KEEP IT CONFIDENTIAL: PROTECT YOUR UNION

I'll take 50 percent efficiency to get 100 percent loyalty.

—SAMUEL GOLDWYN

IN A LOVING relationship, each individual serves as the other's first line of defense. You're on the same team and are responsible for protecting and defending one another. Part of that responsibility includes defending your mate against outside attacks— physical, emotional, and verbal. But just as crucial to your sense of unity as a couple is your ability to maintain a level of privacy within your relationship. All of these responsibilities help to create strong borders for your partnership, allowing you to distinguish between the safe cocoon of your relationship and the big, bad world around you. When that line of defense is crossed because of a verbal blunder, trust is weakened and serious damage is often done.

It would be easy to maintain a strong defense if both you and your partner had the exact same expectations of what should remain confidential, what you should share with one another before you tell others, and under what circumstances you are expected to protect and defend your mate. But every person is unique, having his or her own preferences, personally embarrassing topics, and hot-button issues, so it's unlikely that you and your mate will share identical expectations about boundaries. Unless you jointly create an information firewall around your relationship, you cannot avoid hurting each other, violating each other's sense of loyalty and privacy, and damaging the foundation of trust that love requires to survive.

When you made the choice to be with your partner, you also made the choice to be the person who will listen to her troubles, share your own difficulties, and talk through your challenges together. Part of this unwritten commitment entails being a trustworthy conversation partner who maintains loyalty and confidentiality in two ways: by sharing important things with each other *before* sharing them with outsiders, and by keeping your lips sealed when it comes to your partner's private matters. Unfortunately, many of us overlook these commitments, perhaps because we are confused about what counts as private—or maybe because we don't understand the responsibilities implicit in being our mate's intimate conversation partner. As a result, we often breach our partner's sense of trust.

There are two main ways we do this:

Undersharing: Telling our mate too little
Oversharing: Telling outsiders too much

Undersharing

Crystal is talking to her friend Andrea on the phone when Andrea casually asks if Crystal's husband, Tony, has found any interesting prospects in his job search. Stunned, Crystal can only manage to stammer, "Huh?" Andrea replies, "Tony's looking for a new job, isn't he?"

Crystal can't believe her ears. She feels shocked and betrayed. Too embarrassed to let Andrea know that she was in the dark about this information, Crystal bluffs, "Oh, yes, Tony's looking for a job, but so far nothing has come up," hoping her friend won't catch on to her surprise and anger. "By the way," she casually adds, "how did you know he was looking?"

"I think Tony told Jeff about it last weekend and Jeff told me," Andrea says. Crystal immediately thinks to herself, "Last weekend? Tony had all week to tell me, but he never did. How could he keep something like this from me?"

Crystal ends the conversation and moves as fast as her legs will take her to the den, where her husband is reading comfortably on the couch. She grabs the back of a chair with both hands, looks with piercing eyes across the room at her husband, and loudly asks: "So, I hear you're looking for a new job. Did you find one yet?"

Tony looks up. "What? A new job? Oh, right, I'm just looking. It's nothing serious. I'm just checking out what's available." And then he goes back to reading the paper.

Crystal can't believe Tony's nonchalance. How can he blow her off like that? "So, that's *it*? That's all you have to say to me?" she persists.

"What are you talking about?" asks Tony, sincerely confused by the situation.

"Can't you see I'm angry? And aren't you even the least bit curious about how I found out that you're looking for a new job?"

"No, not really, but if you want to tell me, go ahead," he says, playing along.

"I was on the phone with Andrea and she told me you were talking about it with her husband last weekend and *he* told *her*. So everyone knows but me, your *wife*?"

"That's ridiculous. Everyone doesn't know. I only told Jeff because we used to work together. Besides, it's no big deal. I wouldn't have done anything without talking to you. You should know that."

"I suppose you would talk to me before quitting your job, but even thinking about leaving your job is something I should hear about, from you. It was important enough to talk to your friend about it."

"Well, maybe I should have told you, but I forgot. I told him because I wanted his opinion."

"And what about my opinion? Doesn't it mean anything to you?"

"Well, he knows more about the information technology job market. He's in that field."

"Tony, that's no excuse," exclaims Crystal. "I should still be the first person you tell. I'm your wife! We've been through this before. Like last month, when you forgot to tell me about the dinner you were invited to with your colleagues and their spouses? I had to find that out from Sarah! Were you planning to go to the dinner without me? Or did you think you could tell me a few hours before the dinner and I'd be thrilled to go? Why do I always seem to be the last person to find out about these things?"

Tony knows the conversation is going from bad to worse and he is digging a ditch for himself, so he decides to give in. "All right, I'm sorry. I should have told you those things. I'm just forgetful. I don't do it on purpose."

Crystal wants to press on, but what would be the point? He just doesn't get it. And Crystal is right. Tony's problem is that he looks at each issue—the job hunt, the dinner—as separate, minor issues. Because they're not important to him, he doesn't think it's a big deal if he fails to mention them to his wife. What he doesn't realize is that although each issue may be minor and separate, his reluctance to share information with his wife is symptomatic of a larger problem in their relationship.

Tony uses "forgetfulness" as an excuse for not talking to his wife about what's going on in his life. He doesn't realize that in the process, he is losing her trust and sabotaging their relationship. Tony is a good guy who has a bad habit: He doesn't understand the big-picture consequences of undersharing.

My Father's "I Forgot" Confession

My parents, Howard and Ellen, have been married for nearly 40 years, and I've learned a lot from them about how relationship obstacles can become openings for relationship breakthroughs. Here's my dad's take on undersharing.

When Ellen and I had been married for just a few years, there were many things I didn't tell her, mostly because I just didn't think about it, or I didn't think they were important or would be of interest to her. Then if by chance she heard about one of those things from some-one else and asked me about it, I would quickly resort to my reliable "I forgot to tell you" excuse. At those times the pattern was that Ellen would get angry, yell at me for the oversight, and then let it go. But one day that didn't happen.

The day started out as usual. That night we went out for dinner with two other couples. At the restaurant, I innocently told our friends that I had begun to talk to the owners of a competing business regarding a deal to buy them out and expand my business. I hadn't said anything to Ellen about this possibility. Then, right after I mentioned it during the dinner, my wife's friend jumped in to ask her what she thought about the possible expansion of my business. With a tight smile and some hesitation, my wife said she was thrilled and that if the deal was made it would be great for us. But now as I look back, I know there was nothing great about that evening. In fact, it was a horrible evening. When we got home, Ellen exploded with anger. She went on to say that I had hurt her and embarrassed her by keeping her in the dark about the new business and other things over the years, that my omissions made her feel unimportant and unloved, and that she could no longer trust or accept what I said or did.

Her comments hit me like a ton of bricks. I realized that I couldn't compartmentalize my life anymore into terms of "this is for me, and this is for us." I needed to make a serious effort to let her know what was going on in my life, personally and professionally. I understood that I had to learn how to be a couple by sharing many things that I had previously kept to myself as a single man. That night, Ellen let me know, in no uncertain terms, that sharing things with her on a daily basis helped her to know that I cared. So I made some changes. I made a deliberate effort to share more things with her, and this made me a better husband, which has benefited our relationship through the years.

If the "I forgot to tell you" excuse resonates with you, then consider my father's confession your wake-up call. Why? Because not sharing puts into question your partner's number one position in your life and jeopardizes your relationship. When things happen in your day, big and small, mentally file them in the category "to be shared with my partner." If you have fallen into the "I forgot to tell you" trap, get out now. Keep a pen and pad in your pocket, keep notepads in your car, use the calendar on your cell phone, call or text your mate, or send yourself an e-mail reminder to tell your partner about the issue or event at hand. Do whatever it takes to expunge your "forgetting" habit and replace it with a new "connecting" habit.

What's the Big Deal?

If you are an undersharer, you may be thinking, "Why can't my partner just get over it? It's not that big of a deal." If it happens once, then yes, he probably can forgive and forget. But when it happens the second, third, fourth, or hundredth time and has become a habitual pattern, it leads to anger and retaliation. When you tell your mother about your child's school detention or you tell your friend about a potential business expansion before you tell your partner, the consequences run deep. When you undershare, you instigate a downward spiral that:

- **Sours your relationship.** Like Crystal, who found out about her husband's job search from a friend, your mate feels hurt and betrayed when she learns about a decision you've made from a second- or third-hand source. It sends the message that you don't consider her your top priority and that you don't respect or value her opinion.
- **Turns your mate into a liar.** When someone tells your partner something she hasn't heard from you first, you put your partner in a difficult and embarrassing

spot. In this kind of situation, many people will feel pressured to cover up for appearances' sake and lie, pretending that they already know the information.

When you look at it this way, you can clearly see that undersharing is disrespectful to your mate, pure and simple. It chips away at the trust and loyalty that lie at the foundation of your relationship. Fortunately, it's not difficult to prevent undersharing. All it takes is the 5-minute conversation on page 72. But before we get to that all-important talk, let's examine the opposite problem: oversharing.

Oversharing

I vividly remember the night my husband and I were out to dinner with our new friends Jessica and Glenn. I had met Jessica at a mommy-and-me playgroup, but it was only the second time our husbands had met. It was supposed to be a fun night out for all of us—we had a babysitter at home with our little one, and our friends had a sitter for their two young children.

Making conversation, my husband asked Glenn how he and his wife had met. "We met on a blind date," answered Glenn. But he wasn't finished: "And then Jessica wouldn't give up, she just kept calling and calling me, so I had no choice but to go out with her again!" he chuckled. Jessica wasn't smiling. "You just love to tell that story, don't you?" she retorted, making it clear that she'd heard this embarrassing answer before. "Well, that's what happened," defended Glenn. In an attempt to make Jessica feel better, I said, "But Glenn, you called her back—and you married her—so you must have liked her a lot too!" "Yes, that's true," he answered. And then Jessica chimed in, "Then why do you make it seem like

I harassed you? You called me a lot too." Trying to end this conversation before they had a very personal fight in public, I said jokingly, "I don't think we're going to be able to go back and check the phone records, so let's just agree that whatever happened was fine because it worked out in the end!" And then I changed the topic.

Whether or not Glenn was painting an accurate portrait of their early dating days, his choice of words created a cringe-worthy moment that hurt and embarrassed Jessica. Glenn really wasn't trying to put her down—he was trying to be funny in front of new friends. Yet, because Jessica responded with a snide remark instead of assertively framing the issue as a privacy matter in a 5-minute talk later that night, Glenn didn't take her seriously. The result: Jessica was annoyed with Glenn, and since Glenn still didn't know how she really felt, she could expect him to put her in the same uncomfortable position the next time he was asked how they met.

Are You a Traitor to Your Mate?

It's not uncommon to find that one person in a couple is an accidental traitor, an oversharer who reveals things about personal issues such as health, finances, or marital arguments that the other person wants to keep behind closed doors. Maybe you tell your mother about a stupid thing your mate did, or perhaps your partner tells his friends too much about your sex life when you are trying to get pregnant. No matter what the issue is, when one person overshares with outsiders, trust is broken.

People typically overshare for one of two reasons: Either they simply don't know that their partner would want something to be kept private, or they're trying to one-up their partner or get a laugh. Sometimes people overshare with their friends when their partner is not around. They think, "What my partner doesn't know can't hurt her." But that's not so. What you reveal may negatively influence your friends' perceptions of your partner. Why would you want people to think badly of your mate?

Whatever the reason, oversharers continue to disloyally spill relationship secrets because they're never asked not to. Most couples just don't take the time to agree upon which topics fall into the category of "insider information."

The only way to prevent oversharing is to be specific about what information can be made public and what is better kept private. Plan ahead so you and your partner are on the same team, working together to protect each other from being hurt or embarrassed.

The 5-Minute Conversation: Keep It Confidential

Can you actually cure an oversharing traitor or an undersharing, forgetful person? Yes, by using this simple strategy.

1. Set the Groundwork

Say, "Let's have a 5-minute conversation." Ask your partner to sit down with you and say something like "I think we need to figure out what we're able to share with others and what we want to keep private, just between us." Share a recent example of a time when one of you overshared, if there is such an example, so your partner understands the kind of awkward situation you want to avoid in the future. Then continue, "So I think it would be helpful if we set some limits on what we talk about with friends, family, and co-workers. This will help us avoid embarrassing ourselves and hurting each other, and it will prevent us from getting mad at each other. What do you think?"

2. Establish Partner Exclusives

Decide which topics are definite no-nos that should be kept private and never shared with others. Discuss specific situations that you want to stay within the boundaries of your relationship; things like a recent job loss, a sibling's divorce proceedings, or your child's learning disability. Also be sure to cover more general topics, such as your sex life, marital arguments, health issues, finances, etc. Establish a clear zone of privacy so that you and your mate know that these things will not be brought up to others without mutual agreement to do so. You might also want to agree to adopt an overall "if in doubt, *don't*" philosophy when it comes to sharing with others.

3. Show Partner-First Favoritism

Besides your zone of complete privacy, certain other topics always need to be shared with each other first. Explain to your mate that some things might not be confidential, but that you'd really like to know about them before they are shared with others. Make the point that forgetting to tell one another these things is not a valid excuse. Decide which topics are "partner first," such as new business plans, job interviews, child discipline issues, scheduling decisions, and family issues. This way, not only will both of you be in the loop when there's something important going on (preventing the problem of undersharing), but you'll also be able to discuss whether it's something that needs to be kept confidential.

TAKE NOTE

Never assume your partner knows what you want to keep private. When discussing an issue that you want to remain private, say, "Let's keep this just between the two of us."

Troubleshooting Tip

If undersharing or oversharing happens again after this conversation, don't go back to your old ways of arguing or yelling things like "How could you have done that again?" Instead, point out the breaching of the agreement and identify it as a case of undersharing or oversharing. Once you and your mate learn to label a bad habit, it will become easier to recognize and change it.

Whose Team Are You On?

Beyond clarifying issues of privacy and showing partner favoritism, there is another time when the duty to protect your mate is called into action.

What would you do if you and your mate were hanging out with friends and one of them said to your partner, "You know, you're not the sharpest tool in the shed. You don't know what the heck you're talking about." What would you do if your mother berated your partner about his career choice? Would you defend your mother or your partner? Would you stand by like a silent wimp, or would you assertively step in and say, "That was uncalled for. Please don't speak to my partner that way."

When your mate is criticized in public, it is a character-revealing moment for *you*. If you choose to remain quiet and let your mate defend him- or herself, it is possible that you have honorable intentions and want to foster the belief that your mate is an independent and resourceful person who can handle the situation alone. Or, perhaps you think your mate would be embarrassed by your defense. Nevertheless, whether or not your partner could handle the situation alone *does not matter*.

What matters is that you have an opportunity right then and there to prove that you are your partner's protector and confidant, that you are her first line of defense against a stranger, a so-called friend, or even your own family. If your partner doesn't want you to come to her defense in such a situation, then she should let you know in advance. Otherwise, assume that your mate expects you to serve as a protective shield. To do so signifies loyalty and builds trust and admiration.

TAKE NOTE

You should never defend a mate who is being physically or emotionally abusive to you, your children, or someone else. Leave the situation and/or seek immediate professional help.

What If Your Partner Is in the Wrong?

I've been asked this question many times by mediation clients. Am I really supposed to defend my mate if he *is* in the wrong or behaving like an obnoxious fool? Why should I speak up for my wife when she gets into an argument with the repairman when I know her attitude caused the problem? How can I defend my husband against my mother's criticisms when I totally agree with her that he should get a better job?

Well, friends, here's my answer for you: You defend in public, even if you disagree in private. You keep your lips closed and your true thoughts confidential until you can share them privately with your partner. Your goal isn't to create a false image of the perfect couple or partner, it's to give your mate the security of knowing that if he or she is rudely criticized or attacked by someone else, you can be counted on for your steady and loyal support.

Together Forever

One of the greatest things about being in a committed relationship is the sense of warmth and safety you feel inside its boundaries. When you and your partner are a strong team, with a strong sense of where your loyalties lie, you feel protected and are able to open up and be vulnerable with one another. On the other hand, when you don't have a clear line of common defense—when you reveal secrets to others, don't share important information, or don't defend each other against outsiders—you can never fully relax, because you never know if your mate will support or betray you.

Take the time to draw public/private boundaries around your relationship. The more clearly you can define what it means to be loyal to each other, the stronger you'll be as a couple, and the more secure you will feel in your love.

BE MORE LOVABLE: CONQUER WITH COMPASSION

I married her for her looks, but not the ones she's been giving me lately.

MILTON BERLE

LET'S BE HONEST: No one likes to spend time with someone who is prickly, negative, judgmental, and critical. As much as we'd like to think that our partners will love us no matter how we behave, that's simply not the case (remember, romantic love is conditional). The truth is, if you want to be loved, you must be lovable. What does it mean to be lovable? It means that you are supportive and compassionate—not spiteful and judgmental—in big and small ways every day.

Most of us don't think of ourselves as critical people. We're helpful, kind, and compassionate, right? I'm sure that when really big problems come up—your mate is distraught about his mother's illness, or you are upset over a recent job loss—you and your partner are as kind and supportive as can be. But what about those moments when your mate makes a simple mistake and complains about the consequence? Maybe your wife left her umbrella on the bus and got soaked on the way home, or maybe you're out to dinner and your husband complains because he accidentally ordered a salad that contains onions when he hates onions. Even though the mistake has nothing to do with you, you find the complaints annoying, since the problems were completely preventable. You want to shout, "How many times do I have to tell you to keep an umbrella at work?" or "All you had to do was tell the waiter 'No onions'!" How we choose to react in these petty, irritating moments truly defines us and our relationships.

HAVE YOU HEARD?

How you handle your partner's trivial, everyday mistakes can have a huge impact on your relationship. One study asked divorced participants to name the top trigger for their marital strife. Their number one response? The accumulation of minor stresses and irritants over time.

Do you want to live in a compassionate world or a critical one? Do you want to be easy to love or difficult to be around? This chapter will help raise your awareness of those moments when you have a choice between showing harsh criticism and loving compassion. You'll also learn a simple 5-minute conversation that can turn an irritating situation into an opportunity for greater connection and support.

Quiz: What Kind of Mate Are You?

Take this quiz to find out just how compassionate you are toward your partner. For each situation, choose your most likely response. Be honest—don't pick the response you think is "right"; pick the one that is most real for you.

1. Your mate says: "Ugh, the sunburn I got today at the beach really hurts." You say:

    A. "I told you to get out of the sun."

    B. "I'm sorry it hurts. Do you want some aloe?"

    C. "Next time maybe you should try wearing sunscreen."

2. Your mate says: "I can't believe I forgot to take those forms to work today." You say:

    A. "You should have put them in your bag last night."

    B. "Oh well. Maybe you can explain it to your boss and turn them in tomorrow."

    C. "Why do you always forget to do the most important things?"

3. Your mate says: "I'm exhausted." You say:

    A. "Well, you should go to bed earlier."

    B. "You've had a busy week. No wonder you're so tired."

    C. "Does this mean you want me to cancel our dinner reservations for tonight?"

4. Your mate calls you and says: "I locked myself out. I'm at the front door. Can you come home now?" You say:

    A. "No. This is your problem. I have work to do."

B. "That's too bad. Yes, I'll be there soon."

C. "Why do you always forget your keys? You're so annoying."

5. Your mate says: "I don't feel well. I think the turkey I ate was bad." You say:

A. "You're fine. I just bought that turkey."

B. "I'm sorry you don't feel well. Do you want me to get you something for your stomach?"

C. "Well, you should have smelled it before you ate it."

Results

It's pretty obvious that choice B is the most compassionate, supportive response in each of the five situations. I call choice B the love line. In comparison, the other two responses, A and C, are critical and/or indifferent to the hardship your mate is experiencing. They are what I call fight lines. While being indifferent isn't as bad as being critical, neglect is a recipe for relationship breakdown. The more As and Cs you chose, the more time you and your partner probably spend fighting—and the closer your relationship is to a crisis.

A Closer Look: Fight Lines versus Love Lines

When your mate is in a situation like any one of those described in the previous quiz, you can choose to respond in one of two ways: with a fight line or a love line. Remember, if you are committed to improving your relationship, your goal is not to be "right" in every situation—it is to fight less.

Why Do We Choose Fight Lines?

I know, I know, it feels so good to use a fight line in the heat of the moment. Your partner was foolish or irresponsible or should have listened to you and darn it, you want to make sure that he or she knows it. But I assure you that you won't feel good when your criticism unintentionally ignites an argument, destroys a bonding moment, or sparks resentment that stings for the rest of the day. You won't get what you want—an admission of wrongdoing. What you will get is a defensive response in which your mate will explain why it was not his or her fault, and a rift developing between the two of you. It's simple cause and effect.

The Secret to Turning a Fight Line into a Love Line

You may be thinking, "So what? I'm honest and I tell it like it is. That's just how I communicate. I can't change it." Not true. Though you may have the best of intentions, you have a bad verbal habit that is harming your relationship. Honesty is not the issue here. I'm not telling you to lie or to applaud your mate's bad decisions, just to make a different point that expresses compassion, which is also honest. Too often, honesty is used as an excuse to hurt someone. If you want a loving relationship in which you receive compassion and affection, then you must do unto your partner as you would have him or her do unto you. Even if your spouse shoots fight lines in your direction, that doesn't give you permission to fire back. You are the one interested enough in improving your relationship to be reading this book, so you must be the first to take charge and make a change that will benefit the relationship.

To turn your bad verbal habit into a good one, you need to shift the way you think about these situations. The next time your mate makes a mistake and is dealing with the consequences, ask yourself one smart question before you open your mouth.

The Smart Question: "Does This Situation Affect Me Directly?"

If the Answer Is No, It Doesn't Affect Me

The situation may upset you, but it doesn't directly affect you. When this happens, you have no right to blame, criticize, complain, or even make a suggestion, unless you're asked for it. Think of it this way: It's your mate's problem and your mate is suffering as a result. You are not. Don't waste your energy thinking that this is a teachable moment for your mate, and don't be sucked into saying, "I told you so." It's not your job to remind your mate that he or she caused the problem—that will only push the two of you apart. Instead, choose a love line and create an opportunity for the two of you to come together.

Example: The Sunburned Fool

Consider this: You and your mate go to the beach. After you apply your sunscreen, you toss the bottle to your mate, who says,

"Ah, the sun's not that strong. I don't need any." You disagree, but why argue? That evening, it's no surprise to you that your mate is as red as a beet and complains bitterly about the sunburn. You want to shout out, "You're an idiot! You deserve what you got!" But, in a situation like this, instead of ranting, try to practice some self-control and think before you talk. The pain your mate is experiencing from a bad sunburn is exclusively his or her pain. You are not the one who is suffering. Blaming your mate for the mishap isn't going to take the pain away, make him more regretful for the mistake, or prevent him from doing it again. It certainly won't turn back time and make your mate slather on sunscreen. Instead, your critical words may incite an argument. At times like this, all you can do is offer your support and show your mate kindness by trying to help alleviate his pain.

If the Answer Is Yes, It Does Affect Me

Is it okay to use a fight line when the situation affects you? Nope. Remember, fight lines always ignite fights. Think of it this way: When your partner makes a mistake that affects you, what do you want to take away from the situation? Do you want to fight or be happy? If this is a mistake that happened just once and isn't likely to happen again, then let it go. But if it happens often and you think it is likely to happen again, then what you want to do is to persuade your mate to be more cautious in the future. The best way to do that is to use a love line and then, later on, explain how the mistake affects you and talk about how to remedy the situation for the future.

The House Key Loser

Sometimes it seems like our mates operate in a world of their own, clueless about the many ways that their slipups impact our lives. If your partner tends to forget his keys and locks himself out of the house once in a while, how do you respond when he calls you for help? Do you attack him with a fight line like "How could you do this *again*? Don't you realize I'm busy at work?" It's easy to revert to your knee-jerk reaction (especially if he is a repeat offender), but responding with a fight line will only result in a fight. Instead, try opening up with a love line like "I'm sorry you're locked out. Could you wait at the corner coffee shop for about an hour until I can make it home from work?" Remember to keep things in perspective; this mishap isn't the end of the world. If locking himself out inconveniences you and makes you angry, wait to discuss the problem when you are both calmer. Then talk about how you can prevent the problem from recurring and how you will troubleshoot in the future. Perhaps you'll give a neighbor a duplicate key or hide one in the backyard. Try to suggest a few options without attaching blame for the incident at hand. (Note: If your mate's mistake is affecting you in a very serious way, such as if he or she is abusing alcohol or has a gambling problem, then you may need to seek more intensive help from a therapist to resolve these problems.)

The 5-Minute Conversation: Connecting with Compassion

This conversation goes straight to the point. As soon as your mate relates his dilemma and you recognize that he's made a mistake, instead of launching an "I told you so" type of fight line, begin with a love line and, if appropriate, see if there is anything you can do to help. Try using one of the love lines from the list on the next page.

Top 5 Love Lines

1. I'm sorry that happened.
2. I'd be frustrated, too.
3. I can imagine that it was pretty disappointing.
4. That's too bad.
5. I wish that hadn't happened to you.

When your partner responds to your comment or offer of help, listen without criticizing. Your partner will feel comfortable in the glow of your support, and you'll have taken the opportunity to create a loving connection. If the error didn't affect you directly, you are now ready to file it in the "small stuff" folder and dismiss it. Your caring response is what allows you and your partner to move on.

If the error does affect you and it's happened before and you think it is likely to happen again, then wait until later, when the stress resulting from the problem has receded, to explain how the mistake affects you and come up with a plan for prevention. Ask, "What can we do to prevent this problem from happening again?" Seek your mate's input in solving the problem.

❤ ❤ ❤

Love lines give you a chance to defuse an otherwise stressful situation and connect with your partner. When everyday annoyances pop up and you choose to respond with compassion instead of irritation, you'll initiate a loving interaction filled with kindness and understanding instead of a heated exchange that leaves you both feeling stung.

8

AWAKEN YOUR SILENT MATE: PUMP UP A VERBAL EXCHANGE

Too often the strong, silent man is silent only because he does not know what to say, and is reputed strong, only because he has remained silent.

—WINSTON CHURCHILL

SILENCE ISN'T ALWAYS golden. It can be grating, isolating, and downright hurtful. At its worst, one partner's silence can push a couple into extreme behaviors that result in relationship failure. If there's a silent partner in your relationship, the following exchange will be familiar.

> "Don't you have anything to say?"
> "What do you want me to say?"
> "I don't know. Anything would be nice."

Or how about this:

"You're not listening to me!"
"How can you say that? I'm sitting right here."
"Then why aren't you saying anything?"

I can't tell you how many times I've heard a client say, "I feel like I'm talking to a brick wall. I get nothing back." What that means is that one partner is talking more and the other is unresponsive. The partner doing the talking feels like her mate's silence indicates a withdrawal of emotion or companionship. This is a clear sign that trouble is brewing.

Some couples don't mind when one partner is the talker and the other is more of a listener, but most couples, over time, become dissatisfied with this scenario. Those couples need to rework their verbal approach, because if they don't, their communication will only worsen. The talkers will feel compelled to talk more and to repeat themselves to compensate for the silence, and the non-talkers will simply tune out and wait for their chatterbox mate to stop talking.

If this pattern sounds familiar, then you will especially benefit from this chapter. Although you've probably tried to deal with this issue a thousand times before, don't give up. Your efforts at getting your partner to open up more have likely failed because you've been focusing on the wrong person—your partner. The best way to get your mate to communicate is to change the way that *you* communicate.

In my mediation experience with couples, it is often the man who has less to say. For ease of comprehension, in this chapter I will refer to the silent one as "he" and the talker as "she." However, I also want to point out that new studies published in the research journal *Science* and in *Personality and Social Psychology Review* challenge the popular notion that women talk significantly more than men. These new studies indicate that, on average, men and women talk about the same amount. In addition, researchers found that some men are chatterboxes while others use words sparingly, and that the same variation holds true for women as a group. So, it's quite possible that in your relationship, the woman is the silent one.

He's a Man of Few Words

A man comes home from work and says to his wife,
"I had a horrible day at work today."
She says, "Tell me about it."
He says, "I just did."

Can a person like the one described in the exchange above ever change? The answer is yes. If you change the way you approach him, he will change the way he responds to you.

The truth is, your mate may never be the talker you are. Perhaps he was chattier when you first started dating; a lot of silent types are motivated to talk more during the early, must-impress stages of a relationship. But once your relationship became more solid and secure, and he became comfortable with you, he may have settled back into his natural, somewhat more reserved state.

Or maybe he's always been a little quiet. In fact, that may have initially drawn you to him—finally, you met a person who listened attentively and thought your stories were adorable! You appreciated his ideas and suggestions when he gave them, and you believed that your personalities complemented each other well. Now, he talks so infrequently that you're not even sure he's there anymore.

No matter what you thought of his verbal habits early on, the fact is that now you're not happy with his lack of communication. Sometimes you get the feeling that he's just waiting for the conversation to end, and you can't help but ask yourself a devastating question: How can he really love me if he doesn't like talking to me?

There are two kinds of silent partners: The first is a mate who enjoys listening to you and would like to have more to say, but he's become so overwhelmed by your talking that he doesn't contribute much to the conversation. Your verbal habits have, over time, enabled his silence. The other type of silent partner is unresponsive because something is troubling him—maybe a problem in your relationship, maybe a problem at work—and he doesn't know how to talk about it. You know that you have this type of silent partner if he abruptly shuts down. When that happens, mention that it seems like he's suddenly become quiet. Ask him if something is bothering him. If he won't open up, compassionately tell him that you still sense that something isn't right and that you care about whatever it is that's bothering him. Further point out that if you're left in the dark, you'll probably rack your brain inventing explanations that are much worse than the reality. Let him know that if something is up, you're ready to listen whenever he wants to talk about it. And maybe go a step further and tell him that you will listen without offering your opinion, unless he wants it.

The Fix-It Plan of Action

For the silent partner who rations his words, you will need a consistent, well-thought-out plan of action to change the conversation dynamic in your home. The goal is to create a dialogue that allows both of you to share ideas. Not only should you try asking your partner commonsense questions during a conversation, such as "What do you think about that?" or "Has that ever happened to you?" or "Could you give me some advice?" but you'll also need to dig a little deeper to correct your own verbal weaknesses. If your once-enjoyable conversations with your partner have become more like unsatisfying monologues lately, consider that your mate's silence may be a response to your conversation-halting verbal habits.

How does a silent partner explain his silence? I've interviewed hundreds of couples, and when I talk to the silent partners alone, they reveal four major reasons for their weak verbal involvement.

Reason #1: "I'm Not Interested"

"Sometimes I don't say much when my wife talks because I'm not all that interested in the topic. If she has a 10-minute conversation with her mother, she'll spend 20 minutes repeating the details to me, word for word. It has nothing to do with me."

This is a response I've heard countless times, primarily from men. I'll be brutally honest here: There will be times when your partner simply doesn't care about what you're saying. I'm sure you're an interesting person, and yes, your partner loves you, but he doesn't have to be riveted by everything that interests you. I've heard countless women say, "If he really cared about me, he would care about everything that's important to me." Well, not necessarily. Do you care about everything that's important to him— every detail of his work, his friends, every football score of the week? Our partners *should* care about the things and people that seriously affect our relationships and harm or benefit us, but they do not have to care about all the minor details of our lives, such as why your hairdresser didn't deserve a tip or how annoyed you are at your friend for canceling your lunch plans. If our partners are interested in those minor things, that's great; but if it's clear that they don't need or want to know these things—choose someone else to share them with.

TAKE NOTE

A good partner does not have to care about everything and anything that interests you.

The Fix-It Advice

I have two pieces of advice for you. First, I suggest that you pay more attention to the signs that your partner is beginning to tune you out. You know exactly what I'm talking about: those moments when he starts to fidget or look bored and you instinctively utter the infamous words "Are you listening to me?" You probably don't want an honest answer to that question. Most likely, he feels bored to death or stressed out by your onslaught of information. Recognize this moment, and when it happens, stop talking.

Second, you need to learn how to communicate more effectively. How do you do that? One way is to stay away from frothy, detailed descriptions and repetition.

Amy and Robert Go at It

Here's what happens when Amy shares too many details with her husband, Robert.

> Amy: I just got off the phone with Marisa, who returned from the Caribbean with her family. Do you remember

that I told you they were going there and that if she said she liked it, we should consider going to the same hotel on our next vacation?

Robert: Uh, yes.

Amy: Well, she told me that they stayed at the Hilton and it wasn't what she expected. She said the beachfront was small and that they didn't have enough beach chairs for the people at the hotel. She said the pool was beautiful, just like it appeared on the Web site, but there wasn't an ocean view from the pool, so she felt like she could have been anywhere. Can you believe that?

Robert: No.

Amy: And that's not all. Marisa said the food at the hotel was really good, especially the seafood dishes, but the food was too spicy for their son. I mean, he's only 4. So they went to McDonald's a few times to find something he would eat. Can you imagine—they went all the way from New York to the Caribbean for McDonald's. Isn't that terrible?

Robert: Yes.

Amy: So, I don't think we should take the kids there. Maybe we should just make it simple. Maybe Florida is the best place for kids. The airfare and hotel will be a lot cheaper, and the kids will be able to enjoy themselves and eat what they like. What do you think?

Robert: Sounds good.

Amy: What sounds good?

Robert: Looking at different hotels in the Caribbean.

Amy: Are you serious? Weren't you listening to anything I said?

Clearly, Amy is annoyed with Robert for not listening to her. But can you really blame him for tuning her out during her long-winded, detailed monologue?

A better conversation could have gone like this.

Amy: Marisa just got back from the Caribbean with her family. She said they didn't have a great experience. I'm thinking that maybe we shouldn't go there.

Robert: Really? What was so bad?

Amy: The hotel and food were expensive, and there wasn't much for her son to do or eat. Scott ended up eating dinner at McDonald's.

Robert: That doesn't sound good.

Amy: I think we should probably go to Florida. It's cheaper and the kids would enjoy it more.

Robert: That sounds like a good idea. Let's look into hotels in Florida later.

Amy changed her conversation style to encourage more active participation from her husband. Here's how you can change yours.

- **Limit Descriptions:** Wait to be asked more questions or skip it. You will be pleasantly surprised when he asks you for more details.

- **Conclusions First:** Start your conversation with the main point you want your partner to understand. That way, he understands the relevance of the conversation from the outset and will pay attention.

TAKE NOTE

Remember that we have different relationships for different reasons. Your partner may be your best friend, but he or she isn't your only friend, so think about sharing extensive details with someone else who has a particular interest in hearing about that subject.

Reason #2: "I Want to Avoid a Fight"

"I do have things to say, but I don't say them because I've learned that 'yes, dear' avoids a fight. She doesn't like it when I have an opinion that's different from hers. It's generally her way or the highway. She often tells me, 'You don't know what you're talking about.' So, why should I bother talking?"

If your partner says that he feels like you never listen to his opinion, at the very least listen to him now. Something you are doing or saying is making him think that you believe your opinion matters more than his.

Think about how you respond when he disagrees with you. Do you try to convince or persuade him to see it your way? Do you keep talking until he fully understands that you are right and he is wrong? Do you treat the conversation like a win-or-lose debate? If so, you have the wrong goal in mind. Your goal should be to let him have his own opinion and conclusion, unless you are making a joint decision. In that case, you both need to share and discuss your opinions and come to a joint conclusion.

The Fix-It Advice

From now on, when your opinion differs from your partner's, don't override, dismiss, or fight it. Instead, label it and let it go. Say, "It looks like we have different opinions," or "I guess we'll just agree to disagree." Then leave it alone. Don't continue trying to persuade him to admit that you are right or point out the gaps in his reasoning. There is no need for an energy-draining battle of words.

You can also use the moment of disagreement to show your partner that you not only hear his opinion, but also are interested in it. Instead of rushing to share your own opinion, stop and ask your mate a wise question: "Really? Why do you think that?"

Listen to the answer and then, only then, are you free to share your opinion. That wise question reveals that you value and respect what he is saying and want to fully understand what's going on in his head. This is how to disagree without being disagreeable.

Reason #3: "I Hate the Tangent Talk"

"How do you have a conversation with someone who repeats herself and talks endlessly? She relates anything and everything with story after story and goes off on tangents that I can't even follow. Then she wonders why I say nothing."

Being a worthy conversation partner also means that both of you stay on topic. When we move too quickly from one topic to the next, our train of thought is clear to us, of course, but it can lack all sense to others.

The Runaway Conversation

A tangent talker might start a conversation with "I met the rudest customer in the store today." The listener would think he's about to hear what the rude customer said, but a tangent talker doesn't take the obvious route. Instead, she'll tell you everything that led to her being in the supermarket. She'll tell you about how she invited friends over for a barbecue. She'll give you the menu for the night, then tell you what she was buying in the deli department, and include that she was in a hurry because she had to get to the school to watch her son play soccer. Then, if you're lucky, she'll circle back to what the rude customer said in the checkout line.

Another tangent talker might be overjoyed when someone asks him about one stamp in his collection. What does the sorry listener get?

1. A lesson on the history of stamps
2. An explanation about why he started collecting stamps as a kid
3. Information about a mutual friend who also collects stamps
4. A description of why it's great to share hobbies with friends

Realize that your idea of what a single topic consists of may be different from your partner's view. But when he is the listener and your goal is for him to understand you, he gets to decide the limits of a topic. If you frequently switch topics, you've already moved on to something else by the time he has a chance to respond to the first topic, and he never gets a chance to talk. No wonder it seems like he has nothing to say.

The Fix-It Advice

This doesn't mean that you can't talk about more than one topic in a conversation; it just means that you shouldn't move on to another topic until your partner has given some input, even if it's as minor as saying, "That's interesting."

How do you know if you are a tangent talker? Well, it's a pretty good sign if your partner tells you that you are. Another clue is if people frequently ask you what your point is or say, "I'm not following what you're saying" or "I don't even see how these things are related."

If you think you might be a tangent talker, here's a charming way to change it: Humble yourself. Give your partner permission to help you stay on topic. Tell him that you know you have this tendency. Say, "When I go off on a tangent, please let me know. I'm not going to get upset or take it personally." Give him permission to say, "Honey, you are going off-topic right now." When he does, don't get angry. Do take control of yourself and say, "Thanks for letting me know." Then go back to your original point or ask your partner if he has anything to add.

Reason #4: "I Get Interrupted"

"My partner interrupts me all the time. I can't say anything because she doesn't let me finish a sentence. She thinks she's a mind reader and knows what I'm going to say. But she's wrong. It doesn't matter, anyway; she just wants me to listen to her."

People who interrupt may not even know that they are doing it. They have mental listening blocks that shut down their ears and keep their mouths open.

Here are a few common listening blocks to avoid.

- **Mind Reading:** You think you know what your part-ner is going to say, so you respond before he has fin-ished his sentence.
- **Filtering:** You have some thoughts about the first thing your partner said, so you stop listening to the rest. You feel so compelled to respond to his first point that you interrupt him.
- **Needing to Be Right:** You think his point is dead wrong. Why let him waste his breath or your time with the rest of his comment?
- **Superiority:** It's not something you're eager to admit, but you truly believe that you are smarter or better informed about a particular topic than your partner is. You know

that his ideas probably aren't as good as yours, so you don't want to hear him talk about something you think he knows little about.

- **The Fix-It Advice:** If you exhibit any of these listening blocks (or others that are unique to you), today is the day to address them. This is especially true if your block involves a negative belief about your partner. Holding on to ideas that put down your mate and allow you to dominate conversations is a clear path to more serious problems, including a potential breakup or divorce. You can hold on to your listening block beliefs or you can hold on to your mate. Which is more important to you?

The "Talking Rock" Technique

I know this might sound a little corny—we've all seen this method played out comically in movies and on television shows—but using an object such as a "talking rock" really can help interrupters learn to give their conversation partners a turn. In case you're not familiar with it, in this technique no one is allowed to talk unless he or she is holding a designated object such as a rock, a pillow, or another small household object.

In mediation I met one couple in which the wife had a serious case of interrupt-itis, and as a result her husband practically refused to talk. I suggested that they use the "talking rock" method and see what happened. For a week, each time they had a conversation, whoever was holding the rock could talk while the other listened. When that person finished talking, the rock would be passed to the partner. When we met again a week later, the wife admitted that she was surprised by how much her husband had to contribute—that is, when she let him finish his sentences.

The 5-Minute Conversation: Getting to the Bottom of His Silence

The tricky part about this 5-minute conversation is that if your talking habits really are discouraging your partner from speaking, then you risk making those same mistakes as you try to get to the bottom of your one-way communication. That's why it's crucial for you to be willing to take responsibility for your share of the problem.

Start by telling your partner that you want to have a 5-minute conversation. Tell him that you love him, but that you've noticed that he doesn't contribute much to your conversations. You might say, "It concerns me that I do most of the talking, because I feel like you're not getting a chance to express yourself. I want to know your thoughts on things, too."

Ask him if there is a reason why he remains quiet. Then *listen* closely to the answer. If he's hesitant to talk, remind your partner that you care about him and admit that you have some bad talking habits that you want to change. Tell him—and this is key—that he can be honest with you and you won't be offended by whatever he says. If your partner stays quiet during this conversation or says, "I don't know why I don't talk more," then continue by suggesting the reasons discussed earlier: Is he not interested? Does he want to avoid a fight? Does he hate tangent talk? Is he always being interrupted? Remember that for silent partners, any or all of these reasons may prompt their silence. If any of these reasons ring true for him, then focus even more strongly on the fix-it advice for that particular problem.

Allow for Other Communication Styles

If you work on correcting your bad talking habits, you should see an increase in how much your partner opens up. But keep in mind that he may also be communicating with you in other ways. Don't focus on verbal communication at the expense of other ways of connecting.

In *The Five Love Languages,* author Gary Chapman, PhD, suggests that there are five ways that people look for expressions of love: words of affirmation, quality time, receiving gifts, acts of service, and physical touch. Each partner may prefer to communicate and receive love in a different way. While you may feel that your relationship is strong only if the two of you are constantly sharing your thoughts and feelings in conversation, your partner may consider helping you clean up the kitchen or holding your hand on a walk around the neighborhood to be a mark of a loving connection. Being able to recognize and integrate your differing communication styles is the sign of a truly tight bond.

❤ ❤ ❤

If you work on your own communication skills, you should start to see your mate responding in kind and becoming a more active participant in your conversations. These changes are sure to spark a deeper connection and friendship. Be sure to recognize improvements, even if they seem minor. You might say, "That's a good point. I really understand where you're coming from now," or "Thanks for letting me know how you feel. It means a lot to me," or simply "I enjoyed this conversation." Always keep in mind that positive reinforcement generates more positive results.

KICK-START INTIMACY: ENGAGE YOUR BRAIN

Do you know what it means to come home at night to a woman who will give you a little love, a little affection, a little tenderness?

It means you're in the wrong house.

—HENNY YOUNGMAN

IF YOU WANT someone to tell you about the state of your relationship, there are plenty of fun quizzes on the Internet that will evaluate your sex life and use it as a litmus test for the overall health of your relationship. Every detail of your bedroom habits is fair game: Do you have sex more or less often than the "average" couple (who supposedly get some action about twice a week)? How does your frequency compare to that of couples in other countries? Are you meek and mild or crazy and wild in bed?

No one would deny that sex is an important part of any strong relationship. But in my opinion, it's not the only type of intimacy that matters.

Why? First, because everyone has a different sex drive, bedroom personality, and ideal frequency, so a sexual activity survey indicates little about the strength of a particular couple's connection. There is no "right" amount or type of sex a couple should have. What matters most is whether both of you are satisfied with this aspect of your relationship.

Another reason these surveys aren't that useful is because they can't measure the primary factor that affects your sex life: your level of emotional intimacy. This is not to say that a high level of emotional intimacy automatically increases one's sex drive, but it certainly helps put you on a path to the bedroom.

Sexual intimacy and emotional intimacy are different, but they are closely intertwined. While sexual intimacy is about two people making a physical connection, emotional intimacy is all about two people forming a mental bond based on trust, respect, and caring—and great relationships have both. Some people view emotional and sexual intimacy as a chicken-and-egg problem. They know they are related, but they don't know which comes first. Based on my observations and conversations with numerous clients, I believe that for many women emotional intimacy forms the foundation of a couple's bond and precedes physical intimacy. When that intimacy is lacking, couples experience a loss of sexual intimacy. Even if one partner is comfortable having sex without emotional intimacy, if the other partner is not then emotional intimacy must be addressed.

From Love Mates to Roommates

"We used to have sex, but now we're just roommates."

"I barely notice when my partner is home."

"I feel alone even when we are together."

Do any of these lines sound familiar? They are some of the revealing admissions I've heard time and again from my clients. Some say the change started after a dramatic event like the birth of a child, a parent's death, or the loss of a job. The stress of the situation opened up cracks in the couple's emotional bond, and one partner was left feeling alone, overwhelmed, and unsupported by his or her mate. For other couples, the cause was more subtle. Over time, tiny bits of forgetfulness, selfishness, arrogance, tiredness, and cluelessness ate away at their relationship, and their sexual connection. The specific reasons for the disconnection may have differed, but the constant theme was that one partner felt neglected by the other—and neglect kills sexual intimacy.

A Downhill Slide

When your love is brand-new, it's easy to keep the emotional and sexual fires burning. Every day brings you closer together as you learn fascinating new things about each other. The companionship you feel during mundane activities like shopping or eating dinner together brings you great joy. But as time passes and the novelty wears off, you slip into a more comfortable, less thrilling mode. If you're like most couples, you start to take each other for granted. We've already seen how taking your partner for granted often translates into rude behavior (see Chapter 3 and Chapter 5 for more details). But this lack of appreciation slides into neglect, and that can chip away at your emotional and sexual intimacy, especially for women: Whether it's you or your partner or both who need emotional intimacy before sexual intimacy, you must be sure to nourish it in your relationship. If you don't, your relationship will follow a natural chain of events that moves you downhill from love mates to roommates:

Love mates

Take each other for granted

Neglect each other

Lose emotional intimacy

Lose sexual intimacy

Roommates

I'm not a sex therapist, so I won't offer specific advice on your sex life in this chapter. Instead, I will give you communication "love plays" that will help you use your brain and words to energize *emotional* intimacy—which will put you on the right track for achieving more sexual intimacy. If your partner needs a little persuading to join you on the path to a more intimate relationship, just follow the 5-minute conversation revealed later in the chapter. Stick with me and you will learn how simple it can be to abandon those old habits of neglect and replace them with new habits that connect.

The Anatomy of Emotional Intimacy

Before we explore how to build emotional intimacy with your partner, let's talk about what emotional intimacy actually is. The core of emotional intimacy is shared experience. When you stop growing and doing new things together because your hobbies, work, children, the television, or even your cell phone takes priority, the pulse of your relationship weakens.

Emotional intimacy provides the framework that makes your relationship secure and sturdy, enabling it to deepen and move forward. It doesn't take much to keep this frame solid. You have hundreds of opportunities each day to show your mate that he or she matters to you, that your life is better because the two of you are together, that he or she is your best friend and top priority. When these magical opportunities are ignored, the emotional connection dissipates.

So how can you rebuild emotional intimacy? By making your relationship your number one priority.

TAKE NOTE

Notice that it's often the absence of positive behaviors, not the presence of negative ones, that makes the difference. The opposite of love is not hate, it's indifference. It's not caring at all.

It Worked for Joe . . .

Joe had asked his co-worker, Bob, to help him repair his deck, so the two of them went to Joe's house after work. When they got to the door, Joe immediately walked over to his wife, gave her a hug, told her he loved her, and asked how her day had been. After he and Joe finished working on the deck, Bob stayed for dinner, during which Joe commented on the delicious meal his wife had cooked and let her know how much he enjoyed dining at home with his family.

After dinner, Bob told Joe that he was surprised by how much he fussed over his wife. Joe said that he'd started paying more attention to her about 6 months before and that it had revived their marriage. Things between them were better than ever.

Bob thought he'd give it a try. When he got home, he gave his wife a massive hug and told her how good it was to see her and that he loved her. His wife burst into tears. Bob was confused and asked why she was crying. She said, "This is the worst day of my life. First, Billy fell off his bike and twisted his ankle. Then, the washing machine broke and flooded the basement. And now, you've come home drunk!"

Would your partner think you were acting strange if you came home and behaved like Joe or Bob? Would you be confused if you were on the receiving end of so much attention from your partner?

Joe and Bob may be extreme examples, but the fact is, giving your mate the attention he or she deserves should not be something that's out of the ordinary—it should be a daily habit.

The Path to the Bedroom Starts in the Kitchen

Though some people are ready, willing, and able to have sex anywhere, anytime, others need to be primed for it in advance.

With most couples, at least one member—usually the woman—needs priming. This means that whether or not you have sex on Saturday is actually determined by the things you say and do on Friday (and Thursday, and Wednesday). For many individuals, a close emotional connection is necessary for an intimate sexual connection. In other words, what happens in the kitchen can influence what happens in the bedroom (or in the living room, depending on your preference!). If your sex life isn't what you want it to be, perhaps it's because of weak emotional intimacy. Strengthen the connection with your mate by using the following love plays.

30-Second Love Plays

Love plays are deliberate words and actions that let your partner know that he or she is your top priority. Think of love play as the emotional equivalent of foreplay. On the surface, they're incredibly simple, but at their core, they all send the powerful message "I value you."

Though using love plays might feel a little silly or awkward at first, give it a try. The immediacy and impact of the results will astound you. I guarantee that you'll see more closeness and kindness and renewed warmth between you and your partner within days, if not hours.

There are six main types of love plays:

- **A Follow-Up Love Play:** When your mate tells you about something that's going to happen that day, whether it's a meeting, a doctor's appointment, or taking your son to a soccer game, make it a top priority to remember to ask your partner later, "How did it go?" If you don't ask, she will think that you don't care.

- **A Keep-in-Touch Love Play:** If you and your mate are away from each other during the day and you have access to e-mail or text messaging, send a message saying, "Just thinking about you," "How's your day going?" or "Looking forward to seeing you later." If you think it's ridiculous to think about your mate during the day when you're doing your own thing, ask yourself why. Is it possible you've made your own space and independence such a priority that it's damaging your relationship and emotional intimacy?
- **A Pitch-In Love Play:** Offering to help your partner with tasks even when you are busy or overwhelmed yourself is a crucial way to say, "I care about you. You are special to me."

  In the movie *The Break-Up,* actors Jennifer Aniston and Vince Vaughn star as Brooke and Gary, a bickering couple who share an apartment in Chicago. In one memorable scene, Brooke is doing the dishes after a dinner party and asks Gary to help. He begrudgingly agrees. She angrily responds, "I don't want you to do the dishes. I want you to *want* to do the dishes." Gary asks, "Why would I *want* to do the dishes?" Brooke doesn't explain, but the answer, of course, is that she wants Gary to view pitching in not as a chore, but as an opportunity to show how much he loves her. How many of us can relate to this example? If you want to avoid a breakup yourself—pitch in, in the name of love.
- **An Eyeball-to-Eyeball Love Play:** As love becomes a permanent fixture in our lives, we begin to take it for

granted. We assume our partner knows how much he or she matters to us. This false assumption is a driving force behind the destruction of intimacy. With this love play, speak up and say what you feel, warmly and face-to-face, such as "You're really important to me. I love you and I'm happy to be with you."

- **A Body-to-Body Love Play:** When you and your mate are doing something together, whether it's preparing dinner, tidying up the living room, watching TV, or reading a book to your child, take a moment to reach out and put your hand on your partner's back, shoulder, or arm. This kind of touch is just as power-ful as a kiss or a hug. It says, "I see you. I hear you and we are connected." Don't reserve basic touch for the bedroom. Do it even when the kids are around. This love play isn't outwardly sexual, but it sets the stage for when you're ready to take it to the next level.
- **A Pet-Name Love Play:** Do you and your mate use pet names or silly nicknames for one another? It doesn't have to be the traditional "honey" or "sweetie"—maybe the two of you share a special inside joke or know one another's nicknames from childhood or college. Calling your mate by a pet name (make sure it's one he or she likes) is fun, warm, and an inviting way to initiate a conversation. Use it spon-taneously at a time when things are calm. It will instantly put a smile on your partner's face and change the mood of the conversation. A touch of silli-ness, a bit of play, strengthens your romantic connection.

Intimacy Hurdles

Intimacy hurdles are the things that keep us from giving high-quality attention to our partners. In my experience, the four main intimacy hurdles are:

1. Children
2. Work
3. Technology, including TVs, phones, and computers
4. Hobbies, friends, and outside interests

While all of the above are important, none of them should take center stage in your life, leaving you with little energy for or interest in your mate. Be honest—if a stranger observed you for 1 week, noting how much time you spent engaged in various activities, what do you think he or she would conclude about your priorities? Would your mate be at the top of the list, or would it be your favorite TV show or working out at the gym? When you neglect your mate, she will feel neglected—and that's a problem. To fix the situation and put your mate back in the spotlight, you must become more aware of how the other commitments in your life limit intimacy with your partner.

High-Jumping Four Big Hurdles

Hurdle #1: Children

Children are wonderful, but they can certainly wear us out. There's no doubt that kids are a major reason why couples neglect each other and allow emotional and physical intimacy to wane. Bear in mind that children eventually (hopefully!) move out of the house, meaning that at a certain point you will be alone with one another again. Your challenge is to keep your relationship strong throughout the years, independent of your children.

Actress Brooke Shields offered an honest perspective on this topic in a 2009 interview published in *Health* magazine when she said, "Love can produce the children, but it has nothing to do with the raising of the children. . . . Children don't necessarily bring you together, they challenge you." She makes an important point. No matter how much you love your mate, having a child can take a toll on your relationship. In fact, a recent study revealed a shocking statistic: 90 percent of parents say their relationships took a turn for the worse after they had their first baby. And research funded by the National Institutes of Health found that the more romantic a couple was before the first baby, the worse they fared afterward because the change was that much more dramatic. With all the stress and pressure that raising a child brings, having time alone as a couple becomes all the more essential, and yet couples suffer a huge decrease in that alone time after a child enters the family.

Couple time isn't indulgent or selfish, it's essential. Being able to communicate one-on-one, as adults, without interruption offers great rewards. You don't need to schedule hours on end for "couple time," and you don't need to do anything out of the ordinary. You might simply watch a movie together or take a walk around the neighborhood. Use household chores and errands as opportunities for a Pitch-In Love Play. Join your mate on a trip to the grocery store, help prepare dinner, or help fold the laundry. If you view a task as an opportunity to focus on each other, the chore will become less annoying and sometimes even enjoyable.

Your children exist because of your love—it's important that you don't allow their presence to stop you from being "in love" with your partner. The greatest gift you can give your children is a stable, healthy family with two parents who love each other.

Hurdle #2: Work

Work is another common intimacy hurdle. While most of us don't prefer working to spending time with our partner or family, for many people, work is a crucial financial obligation, a means of personal fulfillment, or both. Striking the right balance between work and play isn't easy. If the long hours, stress, or other demands of your job or your partner's job are limiting the good-quality time you have together, get creative about ways to make room for relationship intimacy. Can you turn off all cell phones, computers, and BlackBerrys on Sundays? Can you make it home for dinner on at least a few weeknights? Each couple will find opportunities that fit their unique situation, and sometimes you may need to come up with a less-than-ideal contingency plan until things get better. It's important that couples make a concerted effort to work hard at nourishing their relationship during the limited time they have together.

It's also important not to allow work to bleed into your life outside of the office, because that can make your partner feel ignored and alone, even when he or she is with you. We all know about President Barack Obama's much-reported date nights with his wife. If the leader of the free world can make time for his relationship, you have no excuse not to do the same.

If you work more than you'd like to, be sure it's not a deliberate escape from home life. Is it possible that you are choosing to work more than is absolutely necessary or to devote the majority of your time to other obligations because you're not happy in your relationship and are avoiding alone time with your partner? If work, a hobby, children, or anything else is your escape from spending time with your mate, you must reassess your priorities to save your relationship. Hiding from the problem isn't going to fix it.

Overall, if your situation is temporarily less than ideal, don't ignore the fact that you lack time for intimacy. Put it on the table by telling your mate that you wish you had more time to be together. Simply making that comment on a regular basis expresses a desire to be with your partner and helps to create more emotional intimacy. The Follow-Up Love Play is a perfect way to show your partner that even when you're at work, you still remember what matters most. And if there's nothing to follow up on, then use the Keep-in-Touch Love Play and send a playful e-mail or text message (not a reminder to pick up milk on the way home).

Hurdle #3: Technology

The hours we spend using cell phones, iPods, computers, TVs, and video games can turn into digital addictions that capture our attention and block us from noticing or caring about our mate. And the number of techno-obsessed mates is rapidly multiplying as new devices are invented and old ones become less expensive and more widespread.

We have become automated slaves to the very devices that were invented to provide more freedom in our lives and connect us to one another. Many of us seem to think we have no choice but to check our e-mail every few minutes, grab our cell phone the moment it rings, log on to Facebook and Twitter each day, and respond to every text as soon as possible. Though we sometimes have the best intentions, our bad tech habits have stripped our relationships of intimacy. Even good old television interrupts our relationship time. Sadly, many of us don't notice this tech effect until its force dismantles a relationship.

Is Technology Interrupting Intimacy in Your Home?

Question: If you decided one evening to turn off all the technological devices in your home, including computers, iPods, video game consoles, cell phones, and televisions, with the goal of spending an evening with your partner, would you feel unsettled or bored?

Answer: If you said yes, or even if you had to think twice about your answer, it is a sign that technology is overpowering your emotional intimacy.

Don't be a slave to the digital world—drop the digital shackles! Use these tech love plays to enable personal intimacy to thrive.

- **Turned Off the Phone during Family Dinnertime:** Use the quiet time as an opportunity to get to know each other better. Try playing the best/worst game: Each person at the table answers the questions "What's the best thing that happened to you today?" and "What's the worst thing that happened to you today?"
- **Create a Tech Time-Out:** Establish a 1- to 2-hour window before or after dinner when you allow absolutely no tech-device usage.
- **Designate a Power-Down Time for the Day:** When actress Patricia Heaton, known for her role as Debra in *Everybody Loves Raymond,* noticed that her family wasn't as close as she wanted them to be, she and her husband decided to make their family stronger by temporarily putting in place the rule that they wouldn't answer the phone after 5:00 p.m. Pick the time that works best for your family.

- **Limit Computer Usage:** Set a policy that you and your mate won't get on the computer for a half hour after getting home from work. Use that time to get in touch with each other before launching into tech mode.
- **Engage Your Personal Secretary:** Agree to let your cell phone go to voice mail more often. Remember, you are paying for a computerized secretary, so why not use it?

Hurdle #4: Hobbies, Friends, and Other Interests

Question: If you were given a day off from work or caring for the kids, what would you do?

Your answer might be something like sleep in, go to the gym, get a massage, read a book, go shopping, play golf, or meet a friend for lunch.

Now let me ask you this: What if your partner also had the same day off? Would you have the same answer? How would your partner feel about that? And how would you feel if she chose an activity to do without you, knowing that you also had the day off? If your partner doesn't mind that you'd use your bonus day to do something on your own, then there's no problem. But if it upsets your mate that you'd rather do something without him or her, then you have a huge problem. Why? Because you are prioritizing outside interests, hobbies, and friends over your relationship.

Yes, I know, you're entitled to do what you want with that day. But that's irrelevant. What matters most is that your mate feels neglected, and this leaves your relationship open to resentment and anger. You don't have to stop enjoying the things in life that interest you or never see your friends again, but you do need to include your mate in these activities as often as possible—and join in the activities that she enjoys, as well. In the end, you will benefit not only from having more time together, but also from learning new things about one another.

When you want to do something for a full day or afternoon without your partner, such as going to see a movie with your friend, use the Pitch-In Love Play to see what you can do to assist your partner *before* you go out. It will set the stage for a warm departure. On occasion, it might mean having to delay your activity for an hour or two, but so be it. That's what it means to put the relationship first.

If your mate isn't ready to put *the relationship* in the number one spot, or if he or she doesn't get that there's a direct link between neglect and the dulling of your sex life, use this 5-minute priority conversation to encourage a change.

The 5-Minute Priority Conversation

This is no time for subtleties. You need to be honest and specific about what you want. It's not easy, and this may be a tense conversation, but stay calm. Pick a time when you and your partner are home alone or, if you have kids, when they are occupied or sleeping. Ask for your partner's full attention and have a 5-minute talk. This talk uses the "sandwich method." The two slices of bread are the positives that sandwich the meat in the middle, which is the problem. Invite your partner's feedback between the slices and listen to it carefully.

Bottom Slice: State the Positive

"I love you and miss being close to you. Can we talk about this?"

Between the Bread: State the Problem

"Our sex life is not what it once was, and I don't want to go on pretending everything is fine. I feel like we've become roommates, and that's not what I want. It seems that so many things are taking up our time and energy these days that we don't have any time for each other. I wish things were different. How do you feel?"

Often, a partner will respond with a comment like "I wish things were different too. But what can we do about it?"

Top Slice: State Some Solutions

"If both of us want things to be different, then I'm sure we can change the situation together. I think we need to make the relationship our number one priority. What do you think?"

If your partner wants to hear more, then talk about the love play ideas in this chapter that struck you as things that would make you feel closer to your mate. This is also an optimum time to use the Eyeball-to-Eyeball Love Play and tell your partner how much you love him or her. Depending on your situation, you will also want to talk about the specific intimacy hurdles you face, from children to hobbies to work. But rather than focusing on the hurdle, go directly to brainstorming solutions. For instance, you might need to plan a date for that coming weekend or establish household technology rules for yourselves and your children. If your partner doesn't want to hear more, then do the love plays on your own and your words will ignite a better response from your mate. Try to show your affection through touch while you're working on warming up your emotional bond. Loving gestures like kissing, cuddling, and hand-holding will feed your emotional connection as well as your physical connection.

Making the relationship your number one priority will increase emotional intimacy; however, don't expect sex to follow automatically. You may need to discuss sexual needs and wants and even schedule alone time at home for sex. If you wait for the stars to align for sex to happen, you may never have sex. Sometimes, you just have to do it!

❤ ❤ ❤

The goal of this 5-minute conversation, as well as this entire chapter, is to end neglect and foster appreciation, respect, companionship (all of which are conditions for love), and, ultimately, emotional and sexual intimacy. It takes a conscious effort, a training of the mind, to pay attention to each other and to habitually say and do things to prevent the relationship decay that turns you from love mates into roommates. With love plays and other new communication skills at hand, you're ready to elevate the level of intimacy in your relationship today.

DETER CHEATING: PUT THE "ADULT" BACK IN ADULTERY

The big secret is that there is no big secret. Whatever your goal, you can get there if you're willing to work.

—OPRAH WINFREY

NOT LONG AGO I received this desperate e-mail from a reader asking me for advice. I'm sharing this note with you because it takes you into the mind of a person on the cusp of having an affair.

> Hi, Laurie.
> You're the only one I trust for advice. I'm 48 years old and my wife and I have been married for almost 17 years. We have two teenaged kids and we own our home, are financially secure, and by all rights should be happy.

Unfortunately my wife and I have grown apart, but not through my doing. She works 9 hours a day at her job and has been neglecting me for a very long time. Aside from the bedroom neglecting, the emotional neglecting is the most hurtful. For the past 17 years, I have been putting up with her name-calling, mind control, fighting, and insults, hoping she would outgrow it or change, but no such luck. I, on the other hand, also have a full-time job, plus I cook, clean, do housework, do laundry, iron, go out with the kids, help out every night with homework, etc. She just complains she is tired and never spends any time with me. Over the weekend she told me point-blank, "You're old, you're fat, and who is going to love you?"

Here is my dilemma: I work with this wonderful girl who is nothing but supportive of me, as I am of her. She is battling the same losing cause as I am, but with her boyfriend of 3 years. Ever since I met her, I have felt a distant natural attraction which is purely her inner beauty shining out as my one true soul mate. She is smart as well as down-to-earth. This past Thursday was her birthday and I went all out to give her a special day to remember. I took her out for lunch; I got her a birthday card as well as a small gift. When she opened the card and read it, she began to cry and I gave her a kiss on her head. She was genuinely appreciative that someone remembered her birthday. She stood up and kissed me on the cheek and said that was the nicest thing anyone has ever done for her. At that moment my heart ignited. I felt a chest pain but in a good way.

> Now I pose the eternal question: Laurie, what do I
> do? Do I confess my feelings of love for her and see what
> happens? Do I break away from this wonderful woman
> and continue on in my miserable existence with my
> wife? Do I quit my job or what? Please let me know
> soon before I screw up. Thank you.

It's hard not to feel a little pity for this man—clearly, his marriage is in crisis. But if we take a step back from the "right" or "wrong" emotional component of his situation, we can see clearly that he isn't giving his marriage a shot at repair. He says he has hoped for years that things will change, but hope alone never changes anything. This man has avoided discussing the serious issues in his relationship and, in the process, has become a door mat filled with anger, sadness, and disappointment. He and his wife are involved in a routine dance of indifference, and when they do connect, it's only to battle with each other. Neither one of them has the courage to face the reality of the situation.

Nevertheless, a bad relationship doesn't justify infidelity. We are responsible for our choices and for the conversations we have—or don't have—with our partners. Cheating is the coward's way out.

Cheating Never Creeps Up on Anyone

Did you ever hear of a married woman who walked into a hotel room with a man other than her husband, only to discover that her blouse suddenly unbuttons itself and lands on the chair? Can you imagine a man whose zipper unexpectedly opens, causing his pants to drop to his ankles at a neighbor's house? Of course not. Clothes don't fall off without someone choosing to take them off. People don't walk into a hotel room, a plane, a train, or a house without choosing to be there. And no one consummates an affair without making the decision to do so.

So let's start by putting the "adult" back in adultery. An adult

> **HAVE YOU HEARD?**
> Research shows that in approximately one-third of all divorces, at least one spouse cheated during the marriage. And every one of those cheaters intended to do it.

is an individual with free will who makes decisions every day. An adult is responsible for his or her actions. Cheaters may behave like children, insisting on immediate gratification without regard for the consequences, but they are adults who knowingly choose to be unfaithful, and they need to take responsibility for that choice.

A married client once told me that her affair "just crept up on her." When I asked her to explain what she meant, she said that she cheated because her husband didn't appreciate her. My response to her was clear: Many people are in troubled marriages, but not all of them cheat. The courageous ones speak up before they stray. They tell their spouse that the relationship has major problems, and then they work together to fix them.

"I Didn't Mean It"

In one of his HBO comedy specials, Chris Rock made a joke about how a man is only as faithful as his options. Though it was intended to be funny, this joke speaks to an underlying truth about how many people perceive the act of cheating: If a spouse is sufficiently tempted, he or she will simply find it impossible to resist.

My stance on infidelity is clear and simple: A man (or woman) is as faithful as his character is strong. Cheating is never excusable, and it is never an accident. Each one of us is born with the intellectual ability to curb a cheating impulse. The choice of whether or not we do is exclusively ours, and if we do, we must accept the consequences.

Here's why this issue is so important: If cheating is a choice and not an accident, then we can choose to prevent it. In this chapter, you will learn to recognize and understand the temptations and problems that lead a person to choose a path of infidelity. You'll also learn how to cheat-proof your relationship and keep out infidelity for good (or prevent it from coming back). Finally, if you use the 5-minute conversation to courageously and confidently speak up when your relationship is in jeopardy, you can stop yourself and your mate from flirting with disaster.

HAVE YOU HEARD?

Statistics show that when one partner cheats, a marriage becomes twice as likely to end in divorce.

Pick Your Poison: The Three Types of Cheating

Before we understand the lead-up to cheating, let's get a sense of what constitutes cheating and how common cheating really is. There are three main types of cheating.

1. Emotional Cheating

This occurs when two people of the opposite sex, at least one of whom is in a committed relationship, become emotionally close and provide each other with the advice, support, and comfort that should be provided by one's mate. What makes this cheating as opposed to a strong friendship is that the cheater crosses boundaries by either sharing with the outside friend intimate details of his or her established relationship or keeping details of the outside friendship from his or her partner.

2. Sexual Cheating

Any sexualized physical contact with a person who is not your mate (including but not limited to intercourse) constitutes sexual cheating. It may or may not accompany emotional cheating.

3. Digital Cheating and Pornography

This type of cheating is more ambiguous. It can include viewing pornography in magazines and on Web sites, watching erotic videos, instant-messaging with a person performing in an erotic video, participating in a sex chat room, e-mailing or texting with one particular person about sexual topics, or revealing secrets about your relationship.

How Prevalent Is Cheating?

A 2007 MSNBC online survey of 70,000 adults found that nearly 20 percent of those in committed relationships have romantically kissed someone else. In another survey, published in *Parade* in 2008, 19 percent of men and 11 percent of women admitted to having sex outside of their marriage (and an additional 3 percent of men and 4 percent of women preferred not to answer that question). Of course, people are reluctant to tell on themselves, so experts widely believe that the true number of cheaters is actually much higher.

And let's not forget about cheating opportunities brought on by new technologies. How does the Internet affect our faithfulness? Here are some interesting results from a 2004 ABC News survey.

	Men	Women
Have visited a sex Web site	34%	10%
Have participated in a sex chat room	5%	2%
Think visiting a sex Web site is cheating	25%	42%
Think participating in a sex chat room is cheating	54%	72%

How would you have responded to the survey questions about the Internet and cheating? What about kissing? Is that cheating? How would your mate respond? What about if your mate had dinner with someone of the opposite sex and didn't tell you about it? What about if your mate traded Facebook messages with an old flame without your knowledge? Would you consider it cheating if your partner sent a sexually suggestive e-mail or text to someone?

My Shocking Revelation

When I was first married and I'd get together with other newly married girlfriends, sometimes the question "Do you think your husband would ever cheat?" would come up. My girlfriends would all say, "No, never," or "He wouldn't because he knows his suitcase would be packed and out the door." I would quite confidently say, "I don't know," and my girlfriends would raise their eyebrows as if I had just admitted to a terrible secret about my relationship.

Then I would explain, "How can anyone know for certain what someone else would do? I can only control myself. I can't say what will be in the years to come. I only know that we both work hard at our relationship to make sure we give each other plenty of attention, appreciation, and respect."

While my friends thought that acknowledging the possibility of infidelity was a sign of weakness in my relationship, I knew that the best way to keep it from happening was not to deny the chance that it could happen, but to face it head-on and fight it. I adopted this cheat-proofing attitude right from the start. My husband and I make each other feel wanted and needed, emotionally and physically. If something feels off, we talk about it and fix it.

Cheat-proof Your Relationship

There are two preventive steps that you can take to cheat-proof your relationship. Even if cheating has already taken place, you can still use these two steps to ensure that it won't happen again.

Step #1: Set Expectations

The first step is for you and your partner to have clear definitions and expectations about what constitutes cheating in your relationship. That way you'll never get into a situation in which your partner's defense is "I didn't know you considered *that* cheating." Remember, there is no absolute standard for what is or is not cheating. All that matters is that the two of you reach an agreement about what acts feel like betrayal and deception to you.

A Cheater or Not?

I worked with a couple in mediation who determined that while having an Internet chat of a sexual nature should be considered cheating, occasionally looking at erotic pictures and videos should not. The husband and wife agreed that as long as there was no interaction with the person in those pictures or videos, they were okay with it. Being up front by discussing the topic of cheating is a smart way to reduce anxiety and dodge potential bullets. This husband occasionally looked at pornography on the computer and was anxious about getting caught by his wife walking in on him. Now, after their talk, he was free of that fear, but knew that if he went any further than that, he would be violating his partner's trust. Again I emphasize that every couple should decide their own limits. When you have a conversation about what counts as cheating, you might be surprised to discover your partner's perspective.

Step #2: Better Safe than Sorry

While the first step to preventing cheating is to have clear expectations about what counts as betrayal, the second step is a bit more intricate. You must assume that your mate *will* cheat unless the relationship is satisfying to both of you. And so Step #2 is to make conscious choices, day in and day out, to show respect, not disrespect; appreciation, not neglect; cooperation, not competition; and vulnerability, not indifference. Although we are adults who have the power to choose not to cheat, why not make cheating a less attractive option?

Additionally, research shows that adultery is sometimes a consequence of believing that one's marriage is already in trouble. In a 17-year longitudinal study of married individuals, researchers at Pennsylvania State University found that extramarital affairs were significantly more likely to happen among individuals who doubted the long-term viability of their relationship. In another extensive study, people who reported that their relationship was "not too happy" were four times as likely to report extramarital sex as people who reported that they were "very happy" with their relationship.

If either you or your partner has already been unfaithful, then your relationship may be very fragile, and you are at increased risk for cheating to happen again. But all couples, whether or not they have weathered a past infidelity, should assume it will happen in the future unless they work at maintaining the appreciation, respect, and emotional and physical intimacy necessary for a relationship to endure.

> **HAVE YOU HEARD?**
> Research shows that adultery is often a consequence of believing that one's marriage is *already* in trouble.

The Cheating Setup

While therapists often examine feelings and emotions to help explain adultery, as a mediator and communications expert, I look to logic, words, and habits. My research and experience have led me to uncover five verbal clues that commonly exist in the months prior to an affair. Do any of these clues ring true for you?

Five Verbal Clues

1. More Unresolved Arguments

You may always have had your regular fights about in-laws or child care responsibilities, but it seems as if more and more issues are causing never-ending arguments that are abandoned without a resolution. Your communication is difficult and energy draining. Since you know the problems won't change, you feel hopeless and defeated.

2. Longer Bouts of the Silent Treatment

When you or your mate can't stand fighting anymore, you move on to the next stage: the silent treatment. You don't know what to say, so you just say nothing. You're frustrated and angry and you really wish your partner would come to you and say, "Tell me why you're angry and I will sit down and listen to you." But he or she doesn't, and you reach a stalemate in which you ignore each other for days at a time.

3. Public Criticism

When one partner stops censoring his or her public comments and gets pleasure out of putting the other one down in front of friends or family, a serious disconnect and lack of respect are evident. It's a lot easier to cheat without feeling guilty when you don't have compassion for your mate.

4. Increased Focus on Relationship Inequities

No marriage has an equal division of tasks and responsibilities. Every couple has to find a balance that works for them with the goal of meeting the needs of the common good—the "we," not the "me." Usually if one partner wants the balance to change, he or she negotiates with the other. But according to research, and based on my clients' experiences, once you feel disconnected from a relationship, you often focus on how much you are putting in and how little you are getting back. The inequities loom large and go unresolved, allowing someone who feels that he or she is getting a raw deal to feel that cheating is justifiable.

5. Thinking You're Not in a *Real* Marriage

Clients who have been unfaithful to their partners have told me that before the illicit relationship began, they were saying to themselves or each other, "We don't have a real marriage anymore." There was little communication, or no sex, or no appreciation or respect for one another. "We were like two ships passing in the night" is the cliché one woman used to describe the state of her marriage before she started an affair with a friend. Beyond anecdotes, research shows that when someone already has one foot out the door because a marriage is in trouble, that person begins to think that he or she is not in a traditional marriage. This leads to believing that "the rules of marriage don't really apply to me."

Choose Your Future: Act Up, Give Up, or Speak Up

Where do these five clues lead you? If you identify three or more of these clues in your relationship, then you have to choose from one of the following responses. You can:

1. **Act up** by cheating to create a seemingly more satisfying relationship with someone else.
2. **Give up** and choose to live in a bad relationship in which you or your mate might be motivated to cheat.
3. **Speak up** by being courageous and using the strategies in this book and the 5-minute conversation in this chapter to confront the problems, mend your relationship, and deter cheating.

I strongly recommend that you choose option 3. The other two options will only lead you further down the road of disappointment, pain, and sadness. It's true that when you speak up, you risk encountering a huge onslaught of intense emotions. You risk rejection. You risk a fight. You even risk a breakup. But there can be no change and no reward without risk. The time is ripe for you to take charge and act. The only thing you have to lose is your unhappiness.

The 5-Minute Conversation to Deter Cheating

This is one of the hardest conversations you will have with your mate. Your goal here is to enlighten your partner to the serious danger your relationship is in before cheating takes hold. This conversation is appropriate whether it's you or your mate who may be on the brink of cheating. Don't try to minimize what's at risk here, but do express optimism. Find time when the two of you are alone and ask your mate to sit down to have a serious talk with you.

The Beginning: Target the Good

"I know it isn't easy for us to talk about what's going on in our relationship, but this is serious and I'm not going to downplay it. Our relationship is very important to me. I love you and I want us to be happy together."

The Middle: Target the Bad

Get agreement that things are bad: "We're going through a rough patch with all the fighting, silent treatment, and criticisms. Something has changed for us, and I feel like we don't matter to each other the way we once did. I'm afraid it's only going to get worse. We can't live this way anymore. I think we could be happy with each other again, if we make some big changes. What do you think?"

If your partner agrees that he or she wants to work on the relationship, you can continue: "I think we need to figure out the problem and find a solution." (Note that I do not suggest spelling out the risk of cheating in this conversation, because any mention of infidelity will have the appearance of being a threat.)

Once you've aired the disappointment you each feel in the relationship, it's time to rip the bandages off the wounds. Use the following exercise to pinpoint your problem areas and remedy them. If your mate is resistant to this exercise, ask if he or she has a better idea for how to fix the situation.

The Solution Exercise

1. Take out a pen and a piece of paper for each of you. Draw a line down the middle of your paper, making two columns.

    Title the first column with the words "We don't show each other enough _____."

    Title the second column with "We could _____ to change this."

2. Now both of you do this exercise separately: Fill the first column with words that express what you feel you are missing in your relationship. In the second column, list specific ways you and your mate could remedy the situation.

Here's an example of what your list might look like.

We don't show each other enough _____.	We could _____ to change this.
Loyalty	Stand up for each other if one of us has a disagreement with another family member
Attention	Turn off our cell phones and BlackBerrys at home so we can give each other our full attention
Appreciation	Start recognizing the things that one of us does for our kids instead of pinpointing what isn't done
Respect	Stop contradicting one another in front of other people
Care	Plan something fun for us to do together

The End: Target Better Days Ahead

Trade your lists and talk about them. Are you surprised by what's on your partner's list? Keep copies of both lists and commit to doing the things your mate requested of you. Agree to allow each other to point it out when the other neglects to do something on the list. Ask your mate to add to his or her list anything new that crops up. In addition, both of you should review the five vital habits in Chapter 3 (see page 29) and be sure to make them a fixture in your daily communication routine.

If you and your mate have trouble coming up with specifics or can't identify the changes that need to be made, then turn to this book, read and discuss each chapter together, and let it guide you toward specific things you can do to repair your relationship.

Doing the work necessary to get to better days is no easy task. I admit that this particular conversation may take more than

5 minutes, not just because it requires brutal honesty, but because it also necessitates creating and discussing lists of grievances and solutions and making an ongoing commitment to fulfilling each other's needs.

Finally, to stay motivated as you repair your relationship, it's crucially important that you recognize your partner's efforts each time he or she fulfills one of the requests on your list.

TAKE NOTE

When your partner fulfills one of the requests on your list, take a moment to say, "Thank you for doing that. It means a lot to me." What you appreciate will be repeated.

Can Your Relationship Be Saved?

Many people give up on their relationship because they don't know what to do to fix it. Now that you have the tools, you can bring optimism and confidence to your relationship. If your partner agrees with you that your relationship needs serious repair, then you can be the one to guide its repair. You can save your relationship.

If, however, your mate is reluctant to change or is dismissive of your attempts to address problems, remind him of your confidence in and commitment to the relationship. Describe the qualities you still love and admire in him. Keep in mind that getting a divorce may end some problems, but I guarantee that it will create new problems and conflicts. For instance, if you and your partner fight about money, those fights will increase during and after the lengthy divorce process, when you'll have the same salaries paying for two households instead of one! And if you have children together and you're upset with the way your partner parents your kids, at least now you know what is going on. After divorcing, you have almost no control over what happens when your kids are with your ex. How will that feel? Why not first seriously attempt to fix the problems you are facing with your mate? Even if your mate isn't certain about this hopeful future together, start using the five vital habits every day and the appropriate 5-minute conversations to propel your relationship forward.

The Bad News

If your mate is totally resistant to any of your efforts toward reconciliation and refuses to work at improving the relationship for a month or more, then you must face the devastating possibility that your mate may indeed be in the midst of a true life crisis, may be involved in an affair with someone else, and/or may have made the decision to end your relationship. If your relationship has reached this point, you must broach this subject in a conversation to uncover the truth about your partner's intentions. If your mate is not interested in working on the relationship, I'm afraid this book will not help you change that. Most marriages are worth saving, but not if it means living with someone who stubbornly resists real efforts at change for such a long period of time that you have to lose your dignity to stay together. For help, I recommend that you seek professional and/or legal counsel.

When Cheating Has Already Happened

If you both agree to move forward after infidelity, you must add two more ingredients to the 5-minute conversation: forgiveness and rebuilding of trust. First, the cheating partner must admit that he or she made a bad choice and that it wasn't an accident, the other person's fault, or the other partner's fault. Once this is acknowledged, you have the opportunity to work together to achieve forgiveness and restore the trust that was destroyed. Infidelity doesn't have to be a dead end.

I have worked with couples whose relationships did recover from infidelity. It was a long and difficult road back, but they got there by maintaining faith in their relationship and optimism that they could get it back on track, accepting personal responsibility for their decisions, using new communication tools, setting new boundaries, and discussing the state of their union on a regular basis. Most of the responsibility for rebuilding the trust lies in the hands of the person who cheated. Is he or she willing to cut off all contact with the third party (sometimes that may mean changing one's job or ending a friendship), answer all of the partner's questions about the affair, and accept continued scrutiny of his or her whereabouts? The cheater's poor decisions did tremendous damage to the conditions necessary for love to exist, and he or she must accept that it will take a long time (and a lot of work) to repair that damage. There are many advice books that deal exclusively with repairing a relationship after cheating occurs. You might want to find one that appeals to you.

The Chronic Cheater

Note that a minority of cheaters are simply cheaters to the bone and have a very fluid definition of "fidelity." There's nothing you can do to change someone who doesn't want to be monogamous. If you find yourself in a relationship with a chronic cheater and monogamy is important to you, I suggest you consider ending the relationship. You deserve to be with someone who shares and respects your values.

The Good News

Whether your relationship is in recovery mode, on the cusp of an affair, or simply not as satisfying as you'd like it to be, what I ask first and foremost is that you find the strength and courage to be honest with yourself and your partner. Put your fears and concerns on the table, because if you don't, you can expect your relationship to grow worse. You can protect your relationship and push it uphill only when you face the truth, have a plan of action, and use that plan in your attempt to reclaim the love you once shared.

CRITICIZE WITH INFLUENCE: BARK, DON'T BITE

I never met anybody who said when they were a kid, "I wanna grow up and be a critic."

RICHARD PRYOR

I REMEMBER HAVING lunch years ago with a friend who was telling me about her latest breakup. Her boyfriend had cut things off, claiming that she was "too needy." She asked me if I thought he was right. Realizing that an honest answer could be dangerous, I checked the sincerity of her request: "Do you really want to know what I think?" "Absolutely!" she chirped. I knew I was wading into deep waters, but I told her honestly, "I think you might have pushed yourself into his life a little too quickly." "Why would you say that?" she asked, frowning. I responded, "Well, you were only dating him for a few weeks when you expected him to stop seeing other women and spend the whole weekend with you."

Knowing the ups and downs of their short relationship, I thought I had made a good point, but apparently my friend did not agree. She rapidly followed up with a lengthy defense describing how he had led her on. I nodded and she conveniently forgot my original point and moved on to discussing her ex's numerous flaws.

While most people honestly believe they are open to criticism, when push comes to shove they don't really want to hear anything bad about themselves. I've even spoken with therapists who admit that they have to walk a fine line between telling patients the harsh truth and glossing over potential sore spots just so their clients don't simply walk out the door and go find someone who will tell them what they want to hear.

End the Insanity

Many of us feel compelled to criticize our partner when something bothers us, because we know that if we don't say something about the mistake or bad behavior, we will certainly have to deal with it again. Unfortunately, in the heat of the moment, we usually act on impulse and blurt out the wrong words at the wrong time, and soon we end up in a verbal war with our partner. Usually this episode repeats itself each time the problem crops up because we didn't handle the situation effectively the first time. It's time to end this cycle of insanity.

I have to admit that I found myself caught up in this senseless cycle after our son was born. With a baby and then a toddler in the house, my life had begun to feel like it was in emergency mode all the time. It felt like my husband was moving in slow motion every time I asked for his help. Soon I was barking orders instead of asking for assistance. "Get me the baby's bottle!" "Hurry up and bring me his blanket!" "Go find the stuffed dog he loves; no, not that one! The one in his crib!" The orders and admonishments simply flew out of my mouth.

My impulsive criticism didn't make my husband move faster or get me what I wanted; instead, it made us bicker. One day I thought about the situation and came to realize that a healthy child is generally not in a state of emergency and that I had to relax and stop attacking my husband for the greater good of our marriage. So what if I didn't get the exact toy I wanted my son to have for another 5 minutes? Was it such a big deal? If my back was hurting because I'd been holding my son for too long and my husband was in the bathroom, did I have to start shouting at him, "Didn't you just go to the bathroom? I need you to hold him!"? Wouldn't it have been just as easy for me to wait and put my son down on the rug? So what if he whined for a few more minutes? It wouldn't be the end of the world, would it?

Mostly, I needed to remember that when I want my husband to do something for me, I must make it a habit to include words like "please," "thank you," "would you mind," and "do you think you could," simple words that are meant for the person I love, not just for strangers like a waiter or store clerk. It's true, sometimes my husband does not respond to our son's needs as quickly as I do, but is that really such a big deal? Did I need to anger him, which I often did with my impatience and poor word choice? In the end, my husband and I talked about the situation one night after our son was asleep, and it took only minutes for me to explain to him that when he does something a little faster, it reduces my stress because my son's needs are met sooner. So we agreed to compromise: I would be a little more tolerant and he would move a little faster.

Blow Up or Give In?

A couple that lives with intense bickering usually fluctuates between extremes of blowing up with impulsive criticism and giving in by retreating in silence in an attempt to ignore all flaws. The question that arises most often is what to wear: boxing gloves or blindfolds.

Neither of those items will work in your favor. While it's useful to pick your battles and to use compassion when your mate makes a simple mistake, ignoring everything that bothers you in your relationship will only turn you into a doormat and lead you down the path of being chronically miserable. Yet, at the same time, attacking or diving in without a carefully thought-out approach will only drive a wedge between you and your mate to make things worse. What will work to bring you closer *and* achieve the change you want is a finely tuned strategy that I call rational criticism.

Rational Criticism to the Rescue

Rational criticism is the intelligent way to make something that is imperfect a little more perfect. Instead of the emotion-driven style of criticism that most of us instinctively rely on when we're upset, it requires a more logical approach, maximizing our brainpower to enable us to choose the right words to make our point. Rational criticism is selective, helping us to avoid the top five ways that people overcriticize, and it is effective because it employs the power of praise. Limiting harsh criticism of your partner is crucial. After all, this is the person you love and committed yourself to; you've got to give your mate a little breathing room.

Needless to say, some criticism is necessary for relationship growth and survival. Winston Churchill put it best when he said, "Criticism may not be agreeable, but it is necessary. It fulfills the same function as pain in the human body. It calls attention to an unhealthy state of things."

In this chapter I will highlight the most common mistakes we all make when we criticize our mates and give you a strategy to successfully package your criticism into a respectful conversation that lasts 5 minutes or less. I will also show you how to bypass the roadblocks that could detour your success. By the time you've finished reading this chapter, you'll have all the tools you need to use your words to change things for the better.

The Overcriticizer

Jim and Anna are having a nice Saturday morning stroll through the park, and all seems right with the world. That's when Jim tells Anna that he has to go to the bank later that day to transfer money from their savings to their checking account.

"Why?" asks Anna.

"Because," says Jim, "I mailed checks to pay a few bills last week, and I think they total more than what's in the checking account."

"What do you mean you 'think'?" asks Anna. "Didn't you know what was in the account before you paid the bills?"

"Not really. And it doesn't matter anyway because the checks won't be deposited the same day they get them."

Anna is instantly pissed. "What's wrong with you? Of course someone could deposit a check the same day. Are you that lazy that you can't check the account balance *before* you pay bills?"

"Look, the mail takes a few days anyway. There's probably no way anyone will receive the checks before today. You're so neurotic. I shouldn't have even mentioned it to you."

"I can only imagine what you *don't* mention to me! You're so disorganized and you defend yourself like I'm the one who's nuts."

"What, do you think you could do a better job than me? You've bounced some checks. You suck at math and you know it."

"That's your defense? That I suck at math? Obviously *you're* not very good at math or this wouldn't have happened!"

After going on like this for a few more minutes, Jim and Anna run out of steam and quiet down, both still utterly frustrated. Nothing has changed as a result of this argument, except that now they're both angry with each other and their nice walk in the park has been ruined.

In this situation, Anna took her criticism too far. Instead of being rational and selective, she became emotional and went overboard. In response, Jim also became irrational and said some unkind things.

Below I identify five main types of overcriticism. Think back to the last squabble you had like Anna and Jim's. Which of these might you be guilty of using? How about your partner?

The Wrong Track: Five Ways We Overcriticize

1. Disguising Personal Preference as Criticism

The Case: You can't stand the color green, but your mate insists on wearing his green V-neck sweater to a dinner party at your friend's house. You want to tell him to change his sweater, especially since you're hanging out with *your* friends.

The Verdict: Effective criticism is not about a personal preference. It is not your place to criticize your mate's wardrobe choices, unless he asks for your opinion or he's wearing his sweater backwards or you have a prior agreement that you will give your partner fashion advice because he appreciates it.

2. Using Criticism to Humiliate Your Mate in Front of Others

The Case: You are justifiably annoyed at something your mate did, but rather than discussing it when the two of you are alone, you announce your criticism in front of other people, perhaps even trying to enlist allies to nod and agree that you are right to criticize your mate for this.

The Verdict: Criticize only in private. Criticism in public is disrespectful and always wrong.

3. Using Criticism to Rub It in Her Face

The Case: Your mate agrees that she made a mistake and offers a plan to fix it, but you still persist in telling her how stupid and wrong she was in the first place.

The Verdict: Don't oversell. After you get an agreement, shut up or you may destroy the positive outcome with further criticism.

4. Criticizing Something after the Fact

The Case: Your mate goes to the store to return a pair of pants you bought last week for your son. You give him the receipt you used to purchase the item so he can get a cash refund. When he comes back, he tells you that he lost the receipt, so he got a store credit instead.

The Verdict: Don't criticize something that can't be

changed. Your partner lost the receipt. It's gone. Nothing can be done about it now. Let it go and thank him for returning the outfit.

5. **Correcting a Person, Not a Mistake**

The Case: You know your mate's flaws: forgetfulness, disorganization, gullibility, etc. Every time she makes a mistake because of one of these flaws, you are quick to point this out with lines like "That only happened because you're so disorganized" or "You're so forgetful. You have a brain like a sieve!" or "You believe just about anything people tell you."

The Verdict: Stick to criticizing the single mistake that just happened, not your mate and her overall character. Turning a single mistake into an excuse to criticize a personality flaw is ineffective and disrespectful. Besides, your mate will feel compelled to fight back to defend herself from these unwarranted character attacks, and soon you will be in a heated battle.

Web of Criticism: Anna and Jim's Story, Continued

Anna's criticism went too far in two ways: First, she made the mistake of criticizing the person, not the problem, when she called Jim lazy and disorganized. Second, she was criticizing a situation after the fact. Jim had already paid the bills and couldn't get them back.

I'm not suggesting that Anna was wrong to react to Jim's lackadaisical attitude about their checking account. But she did take the wrong approach by attacking what she saw as his character flaws. Anna identified the mistake, but then built a web of criticism around it, putting Jim on the defensive and making the problem worse. Instead, she should have used the 5-minute rational criticism conversation to get what she wanted. Read on to find out how it could be used in this situation.

Criticism Gone Wrong, and Gone Right

Brooke loves to get her family together every year to ensure that they stay connected. After her parents died a few years ago, she became even more appreciative of family time and often says, "Family is everything!" So Brooke is thrilled that her brother, Jon, his wife, Lena, and their two children have flown from Chicago to Philadelphia to visit for Thanksgiving weekend. Jon and his family are staying at a nearby hotel, but they spend most of their time hanging out at his sister's house with her husband and son.

It's the day after Thanksgiving and everyone is enjoying themselves as the adults chat, munch, and drink in the den. Everyone, that is, except for Jon, Brooke's brother, who is in another room. When Jon first entered the house, he sat down with them, but then he told his wife that he had to check his fantasy football team and left to use a computer in another room. Expecting him to return in a few minutes, Lena didn't mind his exit.

After 10 minutes pass, Brooke asks, "Where did Jon go?"

"He's sitting at the computer checking his fantasy team. I don't know why he has to do that now," Lena says with an eye roll. Brooke lets the topic drop, not wanting to provoke Lena's irritation any further.

After another 10 minutes, Brooke watches Lena get up and walk over to the computer room. She hears Lena say, "Jon, do you have to play your stupid computer games now? You are so rude.

We're at your sister's house and everyone is wondering where you are. Aren't we worth your time?"

"Calm down," Jon swiftly answers. "I'll come in when I'm done."

Lena returns to the den, hoping that Jon will follow her. But he doesn't. Brooke knows that her brother can be difficult, so it's no surprise to her that Lena's criticism didn't change anything.

Not wanting to interfere, Brooke sits down and waits, hoping the situation will resolve itself. Another 10 minutes pass, and the conversation in the den lulls as all eyes seem to converge on the door of the computer room. Now even Brooke is annoyed with her brother. But she thinks she knows what to say to get him to return to the den. She walks into the computer room.

"Hey, Jon, we miss you!" says Brooke. "We have a lot more fun when you're around. I wish you'd come back and join us." With that, Jon looks up, smiles, and replies, "Okay, I'll be there in a minute."

Lo and behold, 2 minutes later, Jon joins the family in the den. Everyone is happier.

What happened here? Lena's emotional criticism was ineffective, while Brooke's warm, rational approach encouraged him to make a change. How can we be sure to criticize like Brooke and not Lena? It's easy once we learn how to use logic instead of emotion when we communicate criticism.

Where Lena Went Wrong

"You Are So Rude!"

Lena was ticked off at her husband. Her emotionally driven words are familiar to any of us who have been in similar situations. Understandably, her statements reflected her anger in the moment. But her harsh approach of calling Jon's games "stupid" and accusing him of being rude accomplished nothing except to make him angry. Pointing out all of the negatives of his behavior did not motivate him to do what she was asking of him.

The Approach That Backfires

When we use emotional criticism, we instantly feel better because it relieves the tension, frustration, and anger we feel. But I can promise that your good feeling will be short-lived because your anger won't disappear. It will boomerang back to you as your mate becomes defensive, verbally retaliates, and continues doing exactly what made you angry in the first place.

Take a moment to think about your usual attitude when you criticize your spouse. What words did you utter the last time you made a critical remark? Did you achieve the change you wanted, or did you reach a boiling point without any satisfaction?

What Brooke Did Right

"Here's How You Could Be Terrific!"

Rational criticism avoids the negative auto response and harnesses the power of compliments to change someone's behavior for the better. Brooke used rational criticism when she said, "We miss you. We have a lot more fun when you're around." By highlighting how good it would be if Jon returned to the den (instead of how bad he was for sitting at the computer), she motivated him to change his behavior.

It sounds so simple, but as we all know, it's very hard to temper our emotions when we are furious with someone for something he or she did. The next time this happens to you, stop and implement the 5-minute rational criticism conversation.

The 5-Minute Rational Criticism Conversation

Step #1: Keep Your Eye on the Prize

When you start to feel annoyed by your mate's behavior, take a deep breath and ask yourself this question: "What do I want to happen here?" For instance, if Lena or Brooke had asked herself that question, the answer would have been "For Jon to come back into the den." Being aware of a specific goal will help you keep your emotions in check and prevent you from saying or doing anything that will work against that goal.

Step #2: Sweeten the Deal

Now that you know what your goal is, think about the positive reasons why you want it to happen. For instance, if Lena had focused on the fact that she enjoyed Jon's company instead of how rude he was for isolating himself, she would have approached their conversation differently.

Step #3: Say What You Want, Not What You Don't Want

State your criticism with kindness, not accusation. After pointing out the positive side of what you want, stop there. There is no need to say anything bad about the person or what he or she did. When your partner makes the change you seek, it's a good idea to acknowledge it.

More 5-Minute Conversations in Action

Let's review two more examples of how this 5-minute rational criticism conversation would work.

Example #1: Anna and Jim

Anna attacked her husband, Jim, because he nearly overdrew on their checking account, which started a huge fight between them. Here's how she could have used the 5-minute rational criticism conversation to resolve the situation.

1. **The Goal:** To make sure the checking account balance is always sufficient to pay monthly bills
2. **The Positive:** "It would be so great if we could pay bills and write checks for small things without being concerned about it."
3. **What You Want:** "Since our monthly bills are pretty standard, why don't we work it out to have a minimum balance in the checking account at all times? How about if we set up a standard transfer at the beginning of the month, or have one of our paychecks direct-deposited in the checking rather than the savings account?" Next month, when the minimum balance is in place, Anna should point out that their plan is working.

Example #2: You Ruined the TV!

Imagine that while you were out, your partner unsuccessfully tried to use the remote to switch from the TV to the DVD player and ruined the television picture and quality.

"You did that again?" you ask. "The last time you pressed all those buttons it took me an entire night to readjust the TV! What's wrong with you? Why couldn't you wait for me to get home?" Naturally, this leads to a silly fight about the television remote and your mate's ineptitude when it comes to electronics. Nothing good comes of your criticism.

The 5-minute rational criticism conversation using the three steps would go like this.

1. **The Goal:** To have your partner know how to use the remote correctly
2. **The Positive:** "It would be great if you knew how to use the remote yourself so you could do whatever you want with the TV whenever you want to."
3. **What You Want:** "Why don't I write down some simple directions for how to switch between DVD and the television so that when I'm out, you don't have to worry about it. Does that work for you?"

Roadblocks: Defensive Maneuver Alert

Be prepared that even with rational criticism your mate may react with one of the following defensive maneuvers. If you hear any of these, don't get sucked into an argument.

Denial: "I didn't do that." "You're wrong."
Excuses: "The train was late." "I was too exhausted."
    "I didn't do it on purpose."
Sarcasm: "What? Since when are you so perfect?"
Blaming: "If you hadn't done X, I wouldn't have done Y."
Justification: "What else was I supposed to do?" "I did the
    right thing."

The Higher-Road Response

When you hear one of these defenses or something similar, it's a red flag that too many negative words may have seeped into your criticism. Shift gears and go for 100 percent positive with this comment: "Wait. Maybe I have it wrong. I understand that what's done is done. I'm just thinking about how to make it easier for both of us in the future." Wait for a nod or a comment like "Okay, I'm all for that." Then, head back to the three steps. If necessary, repeat the same higher road comment when things get hairy again.

Disarming the Critic

What if your mate uses emotional criticism? How can you neutralize the anger and end the attack?

If your mate misuses criticism or negatively attacks you in any way, try using one of the following comments to turn the conversation to a more positive note:

"I'll definitely consider what you said."
"I understand where you're coming from."
"I didn't mean to upset you."
"I can tell you're angry, and I don't want to fight. Do you want to talk about this when we are calmer?"
"I'd rather talk about how we can prevent this from happening again. Here's my idea...."

Even if your mate is attacking something worthy of criticism, that doesn't mean you should suffer from hearing purely negative comments. Once your mate calms down, let him or her know that you would be so much more open to the advice if he or she would just focus on a solution to the problem instead of yelling about it.

❤ ❤ ❤

The basic theory behind rational criticism is simple: Engage your brain and subdue your emotions. If you're stuck in a cycle of emotional criticism, you already know that it's unproductive and ineffective. Get real with yourself. Pay serious attention to the aftermath of one of your explosions—doing so will help you understand the importance of turning down your emotions and turning up your logic. Make a deliberate decision today to make each word count so your criticism influences your mate to change for the better. By using positive words to your advantage, you will display the respect that is necessary for love to flourish, and you will also attain the change you seek.

REJECT STUBBORNNESS: GET OUT OF YOUR OWN WAY

Stubbornness and stupidity are twins.

—SOPHOCLES

IMAGINE THAT YOU'RE sitting at the computer while your wife is in the kitchen preparing dinner. You're trying to watch an online video, but you hear her yelling something. You turn your ear toward the door and try to decipher what she's saying. She shouts again, this time a little louder. It sounds like a request and it seems to be directed at you, but you still can't make out most of her words.

You yell back, "I can't hear you," and continue watching and listening to the video a friend forwarded to you. If it's important, you figure she'll come in and tell you what it is. She yells again, and this time you can hear her say, "Do you know where." But the rest? Nothing.

So you lean back in your chair and tilt your head in an effort to move your ear closer to the kitchen. "Do I know where *what* is?" you yell.

But now she is at the door of your office yelling, "The salt, you jerk! The salt! Couldn't you get off your behind and come into the kitchen to see what I wanted? You know I'm in the middle of cooking dinner!"

Okay, maybe your wife could have walked over to you right from the start and eliminated the cause of the bickering. But she didn't. Maybe her hands were full, or she couldn't leave a boiling pot unattended on the stove. In that first moment of hearing her incomprehensible yell, you had a choice: You could either focus on what she could have done (walked over to you) or focus on what you could do to change the situation (go to her).

How many times have you stubbornly sat on your butt, refusing to budge while your mate calls for you from another room? We're all a little stubborn sometimes. And it's that attitude of sticking to our position (because we know we're right, or we're angry or just lazy and comfortable sitting down) that keeps us locked in place, physically and mentally.

Of Two Mind-Sets

A relationship can't function well when one partner fails to consider the possibility that some problems may not be entirely the other partner's fault. How we view any given situation or issue determines whether we will find a solution or block one from surfacing. And in every case, we can choose to be closed and stubborn or flexible and open-minded.

If we decide to let a stubborn mind-set direct us, we quickly point the finger at others—"It's not my fault. It happened because of you," or "I'm right, you're wrong. I know what's best." This kind of stubbornness is often rooted in reckless pride or an inflated ego, and it makes it hard for us to see the truth or make wise decisions. And this disrespectful, intolerant, and downright ignorant attitude encourages our mates to respond with bitterness and hostility.

On the other hand, if we choose to adopt a flexible, humble mind-set, allowing for self-reflection and thoughtful consideration of our mate's ideas—"Yes, maybe I play a part in this problem," "Actually, she has a good point"—then we will become a better partner, and a more likable one. We'll also have a smarter perspective on our problems, and we'll make better decisions overall, because seeing things from multiple viewpoints is what makes a person wise.

If your partner is the stubborn one, then you will need to have the 5-minute conversation presented later in this chapter. But if you're the one with the stubbornness problem, then it's up to you to make a clear, conscious decision today to lose the bad attitude and get out of your own way. Try these six simple opportunities for rejecting stubbornness and put yourself on the path to becoming a better partner.

Six Opportunities for Rejecting Stubbornness

Opportunity #1: Discover the Power of "Maybe"

Do you have a habit of instantly saying or thinking, "No, you're wrong" or "I've heard all that before"? The next time you experience that negative response to something someone says or does, stop yourself and think about whether there is any chance that someone else could have a valid point of view. If there is, then quickly replace your "no" with a "maybe." Not only does the word "maybe" show you're open to options, just using the word automatically opens up your mind. Listen while your partner talks. Your understanding and knowledge will grow, and you will make a wiser decision as a result. A little bit of "maybe" goes a long way.

Opportunity #2: Replace "You Should Have" or "You Could Have" with "I Can"

Do you often find yourself thinking things like "She should have remembered to buy more toilet paper when she went to the drugstore yesterday" or "He could have cleared the snow in the driveway last night before it froze and made the driveway slippery"? "Should" and "could" are our mind's way of passing the buck to someone else. Rather than being stubborn and focusing on what your mate *should* have done, focus on yourself and what you *can* do in the present to make a situation better. Can you go the drugstore to pick up more toilet paper? Can you put salt on the driveway to defrost it? When you choose to think about what can be done instead of what should have been done, your openness will lead you to a better outcome: a solution, and no fight.

Opportunity #3: Scrap the Competition

Do you think you're smarter than your mate? Do you think you have a better memory? Do you look for opportunities to prove your superiority? Why? Of course you're better than your mate at certain things. But you're never going to be better than him or her at *everything*. And if you're always busy looking for opportunities to show up your mate, then you'll be blind to the many opportunities to show off your mate and learn from his or her strengths. As Will Rogers wisely put it, "We are all ignorant, only on different subjects."

Opportunity #4: Forget the Word "Everyone"

Too many people dig in their heels by using "everyone" to prove their point. You might say, "Everyone does it" or "Everyone knows that" or "Everyone else agrees with me, so you must be wrong." When we suffer from stubbornness, many of us make a last-ditch effort to prove our point by calling upon the phantom forces of "everyone" for support. But "everyone" doesn't live with you, so it doesn't matter what "everyone" thinks. What does matter is what you and your mate think, and what works best for your relationship.

Opportunity #5: Let Go of a Stubborn Grudge

What is a grudge? It's a decision to have an unforgiving spirit and to dwell on a problem that may or may not be resolved. It's choosing to believe that you have been wronged and that your position is 100 percent right. You want this person to beg, plead, and suffer, and the more the better. In fact, even when your mate does something new and redeeming, you turn it against him or her with a comment like "It would have been nice if you had done that the last time I needed you to do it. It doesn't matter now." Carrying a grudge may seem to give you instant attention and a feeling of superiority. Unfortunately, the person who suffers the most is you. A grudge is a heavy thing to carry around. Let it go! Choose to get better instead of staying bitter.

Opportunity #6: Make Something Temporary

When the winds of stubbornness surround you and it feels like torture to agree to an idea that's not your own, make it temporary, not permanent. Tell yourself and your mate that you will try this other way, do this other thing, temporarily. Say that you will test it and that you reserve the right to reconsider. Give yourself wiggle room to change your mind. It is a smart way to take a small step in the move from stubbornness toward flexibility.

Hearing Isn't Listening

Nature hath given men one tongue but two ears, that we may hear from others twice as much as we speak.
—EPICTETUS

Not only do you want to use the six opportunities to rein in your stubbornness, it's also a good idea to listen first and talk second when you're communicating with your mate in everyday situations. This forces even the most stubborn person to consider his or her mate's perspective. Mediators use three valuable strategies with their clients to make sure they aren't just hearing (that's when words go in one ear and out the other), but rather are listening closely (that's when the listener actually thinks about what is being said). Use these techniques the next time you talk to your partner and you will inspire a more satisfying conversation for both of you.

1. **Add Encouraging Comments:** Don't sit there with a blank expression on your face. Do include words and comments like "That's interesting," "Really?" "Hmm," "I hadn't thought of that," and "That's a good idea" after your partner shares his or her opinion.

2. **Ask Open-Ended Questions:** Rather than asking a closed question like "Did you do this?" or "Did that really happen?"—which will yield a "yes" or "no"

answer—ask an open-ended question like "What do you think?" "How do you think he should have handled it?" or "Why do you think that happened?"

3. **Paraphrase:** When your spouse offers an opinion about something, don't dismiss the comment or contradict him or her right away. Instead, paraphrase what was said. For example, "So, you don't think we should get a new computer right now because you want to wait for the new version of Windows to come out." Paraphrasing forces you to put your own opinion on hold as you let your partner know that you are listening.

What If Your Mate Refuses to Listen?

A good listener is not only popular everywhere, but after a while he gets to know something.

—WILSON MIZNER

Your mate's stubborn attitude sends an unspoken message: "I don't respect what you have to say. You don't matter to me. I'm in charge." It feels awful to be on the receiving end of that. Little by little, this message works to destroy the mutual respect, compassion, and spirit of teamwork necessary for a relationship to survive.

I could give you tips on how to handle stubbornness one situation at a time. I could easily encourage you to let the small things go. But that advice has limited value in dealing with the bigger issue—the constant, gnawing feeling that your voice is not being heard.

So what do you do? How do you persuade your mate to include your thoughts and exclude those closed-minded, self-centered, knee-jerk responses to daily occurrences? You use the following 5-minute conversation.

The 5-Minute Conversation to Halt a Stubborn Mate

Choose a time when both of you are calm and not in the midst of an argument. Ask your mate to sit across from you at the table so you are face-to-face. Then:

1. Rewind the Past

"I think both of us can be stubborn sometimes and it often leads us into a fight. It's such a waste of our energy. We've got to make a change and start listening to each other before our stubborn patterns get worse." Then, share an example, such as "Remember the other day, when I wanted to stop at the supermarket and you didn't, you said no and you wouldn't say why? You refused to listen to my reasons for wanting to make a supermarket stop. I was so annoyed, but I held my tongue the rest of the way home. If you had given me a chance to explain myself, you might have changed your mind. Can you understand that?" Listen to your mate's response and guide the conversation to Steps 2 and 3.

2. Discuss the Present

"Your opinions matter to me. And when we listen to each other and talk calmly like we're doing right now, I feel like we're connecting and that what I say matters to you. Shouldn't it be that way all the time?"

3. Determine the Future

"Here's what I'm thinking: From now on, why don't you stop me and actually tell me I'm being stubborn if you think I'm reacting to something without first listening to you. I also want to be able to tell you when you are doing that, too. Let's promise each other not to get mad when we do this. It's kind of ridiculous for either of us to think we know what's best all the time."

Nurture Open-Mindedness

The next time your mate's stubborn attitude pops up, try to keep your tone light, and remind him or her of the pact you made during the 5-minute conversation. Then share your opinion, assuming that your mate is willing to abide by your agreement. End your verbal exchange on a high note of praise. Acknowledge the positive change in your mate's response and express how much better you feel when your concerns and opinions are given respect.

Whether you or your partner is the stubborn one in your relationship, ending the habit of digging in your heels will broaden your conversations, allowing you to see new qualities and strengths in your mate. You'll also suddenly see the potential for new solutions and compromises (and so will your mate). When you keep an open mind and encourage your mate to do the same, the world becomes bigger and more interesting.

13

ORCHESTRATE A PERFECT APOLOGY: MAKE MUSIC FOR YOUR EARS

A stiff apology is a second insult. . . . The injured party does not want to be compensated because he has been wronged; he wants to be healed because he has been hurt.

—G. K. CHESTERTON

"LOVE MEANS NEVER having to say you're sorry" is probably the most famous line from *Love Story*, the 1970 film starring Ali MacGraw and Ryan O'Neal. To me, that line is horribly misleading, as bad as the myth that love should be unconditional.

As we've seen, certain conditions are necessary for love to survive: appreciation, respect, compassion, trust, and companionship. If any one of those conditions isn't met, love cannot endure. That's why the act of apologizing is essential. A perfect apology offers an acknowledgment that a line has been crossed, causing one or more of those conditions to be threatened or

violated, and it provides a way for you to move back to the right
side of that line together.

The Bad Apology

Giving no apology for a relationship wrongdoing is unacceptable,
but an ill-thought-out apology can be just as destructive. We all
know a bad apology the minute we hear it.

> "Okay, okay, I'm sorry!" she says hurriedly—but you
> get the sense that she doesn't even know what she's sorry
> about and is just saying whatever it will take to get you off
> her back.
> *Or:*
> "Fine, I'm sorry. I won't do it again," he says—but he's made
> the same promise numerous times before, and yet he contin-
> ues to make the same mistake over and over.

A bad apology comes across as insincere and unbelievable. It
can actually make the situation worse, because instead of repairing the damage, it further erodes trust.

Love Means Having to Say You're Sorry—The Right Way

Time and again in my mediation practice, I've seen people who
are truly sorry for something they've done but have trouble con-
veying their regret because of poor verbal skills. Many people
don't know how to choose the right words to effectively express
their remorse. Instead, in the heat of the moment, they blurt out
words that add fuel to a raging fire.

If you and your mate have trouble with apologies, it's time to
change the way you think about saying "I'm sorry." Simply put, if

we can assume that you're both good people who love each other and want to remain a couple, your bad apologies are a communication problem, *not* a people problem. Some people have the best intentions, but they just don't know the right words to express them. As a result, many couples suffer through longer and harsher fights than are necessary.

While each type of mistake requires a different intensity of remorse, there is a standard technique everyone can use to give a perfect apology. It requires no more than 5 minutes and works 100 percent of the time.

The 5-Minute Conversation: The Perfect Apology Technique

A perfect apology between you and your mate is a verbal bridge that acknowledges the way that an action or comment violated one or more love conditions. This technique has three simple parts: the beginning, the middle, and the end. Each part requires only a minute or two of conversation. In total, you need to spend about 5 minutes to attain forgiveness. Toward the end of this chapter you will find out how to use your newly acquired apology skills to guide your partner, who may not have read this chapter, into giving you the expression of remorse that you deserve when he or she makes a mistake that distresses you.

TAKE NOTE

If you want to apologize for something, but you're running out the door in the morning and don't have 5 minutes to spare, you could send a quick e-mail or text message or make a phone call during the day to let your partner know that you regret the way you left things and want to talk later.

The Beginning: Turn a Molehill into a Mountain

Yes, you read that right. I'm asking you to make a small offense appear bigger.

When you are first made aware of your mistake, it's very important that you use the moment to start the apology off on the right foot. That's why you need to begin by making your apology bigger than the crime.

People who make bad apologies have a tendency to diminish their errors, perhaps in an effort to feel less guilty about their error. But minimizing the damage done to your partner will only further upset her.

Don't make diminishing comments like:

"It's not a big deal."
"I really didn't mean it."
"You're overreacting."
"What difference does it make anyway?"
"You're blowing everything out of proportion."

No matter how small you believe your mistake actually was, your partner is always going to feel that it was significant. Nothing will make your partner happier than knowing that you understand how much your mistake impacted him or her.

Do make embellishing comments like:

"I made a big mistake."
"I never should have done that."
"That was so thoughtless of me."
"You didn't deserve that."

"I should have known better."

"I can't believe I acted so selfishly."

By acknowledging that your mistake was a big deal, you are showing an appropriate level of remorse. When your mate can see that you are genuinely remorseful, he or she is much more likely to accept your apology and be willing to move on.

The Middle: Dig Deep

Admit Your Real Wrong

This is the heart of the perfect apology and the spot where many people fail. Sometimes we're quick to own up to the superficial part of a mistake, like forgetting to do something we'd promised to do or making a careless remark. But these are just symptoms of a larger offense we've committed. For our apology to match the magnitude of our error, we must acknowledge the larger breach underlying the mistake.

As I mentioned earlier, your mistakes harm your relationship because they threaten one or more of the conditions necessary for love to thrive (appreciation, respect, compassion, trust, and companionship). In order to offer a perfect apology, you must know and acknowledge which conditions and other values you have undermined with your actions.

For example, let's say you came home late from work, having forgotten that you had agreed to come home early to go out to dinner with your wife's friend and her husband.

A bad apology would be "I'm sorry I forgot about our dinner plans." This only touches on the surface of the mistake.

A perfect apology digs deeper to reveal how the mistake threatened a love condition, such as trust. "I'm sorry I forgot about our dinner plans with the Smiths because I know you were disappointed and embarrassed to have to cancel at the last minute. I'm sorry that I didn't follow through on a promise I made to you."

Or, if you said something rude to your mate in the middle of a fight and you regret your words, don't just say, "I'm sorry I said that to you." A perfect apology would include "I'm sorry I said that because it was mean and disrespectful. No matter what is going on between us, I should never blurt out something hurtful. I am supposed to protect you, not hurt you." Using the word "because" in the first sentence of your apology enables you to dig deeper and explain how you hurt your partner.

TAKE NOTE

A perfect apology includes the word "because." Say "I'm sorry *because*" and list the ways that you hurt your partner.

No Buts about It

A perfect apology never, ever includes a "but." In the above example, a terrible apology would be "I'm sorry I'm late, but you should have called to remind me." Or "I'm sorry that I forgot, but work was really busy and I have a lot on my mind." A "but" is really a disguised effort to deflect blame. It's saying "It's not my fault."

The End: Repair and Prevent

After you've admitted the depth of your mistake, the perfect apology technique requires an ending that aims to repair the damage and prevent the mistake from happening again.

Repair the Damage

In repair mode, you talk about what you could do to make the situation a little better. For instance, in the previous situation, good repair work would be to call the friends to reschedule and let them know that you are sorry for inconveniencing them.

There are times when your mistake is irreparable, such as when you overshare the details of something that your mate wanted to keep between the two of you. After you acknowledge that your mistake violated your partner's privacy and put your loyalty and trust into question, you should skip repair because you can't take back your words. In a situation like this, move straight from apology to prevention, as detailed below.

Prevent a Rerun

The last step in a perfect apology is to craft a prevention plan. Einstein famously remarked that the definition of insanity is "doing the same thing over and over again and expecting a different result." Well, a prevention plan is how you make a change and get a better result.

Your apology is much more likely to be accepted if you can explain to your partner how you will ensure that you won't make the same mistake again and—this is crucial—if you follow through on that plan as time passes.

For example, if you have to apologize for forgetting dinner plans with friends, then your prevention plan could be "In the future, when we have plans that require me to come home early, I will call you that afternoon so you know that I remember." Or, if you said something offensive to your mate in the heat of the moment, you could offer this plan: "In the future, when I start to get heated, I'm going to ask you to give me 5 minutes alone to cool down."

When you offer a prevention plan, you display thoughtfulness and sincerity in your desire to be a better partner to your mate.

No Makeup Gifts: Don't Dilute Your Apology

Many people have a habit of giving gifts to say they're sorry. In fact, it's become such a common way to apologize that when my husband came home with a bouquet of flowers for me one evening, the doorman for our apartment building asked, "Hey, what did you do wrong?"

Giving your partner flowers, a store-bought "I'm sorry" card with a quick signature at the bottom, or any other tangible makeup gift as a way to repair and seek forgiveness is a cop-out. It is a distraction that might momentarily lift the mood in your house, but when that temporary glow wears off, you will have missed your opportunity to give a perfect apology. Instead of showing that you understand what you did wrong and how it hurt your partner, all you will have proven is that you know how to use your credit card.

Even if you do apologize in addition to giving a present, adding a gift cheapens the apology by making it seem like you're trying to bribe your partner. A gift is contaminated when it is used as a get-out-of-jail card. If you really want to give your partner a gift or a loving greeting card, buy it now but give it later, when the gift won't have any connection to the apology. Trust me, the gift of flowers or anything else will be much more appreciated when it's given without strings attached.

The Other Side of the Coin

To err is human, to forgive divine.
— ALEXANDER POPE

TAKE NOTE

If your partner is so angry that he won't listen to anything you have to say, give him a few hours to cool down and then say, "I know you are angry, and I am upset because it's my fault. Can I please talk to you so that I can apologize?"

I have no doubt that you, as well as your partner, will be guilty of many blunders over time. But what if your mate hasn't read this chapter and you're the only one with knowledge of the perfect apology technique? What good will that do when your mate messes up? Assuming that your mate wants to fix the situation, you can help guide him or her into saying exactly what you need to hear.

Be an Apology Coach

I must tell you that you won't get a 100 percent perfect apology by coaching your mate, because you are going to have to fill in a few gaps. But you will receive an acceptable apology, and you will be able to forgive and move on.

First, coach your mate into recognizing that what occurred is a big deal. Say, "I know that your mistake isn't the end of the world, but what you did affected me in a big way. Can you understand that?" Second, ask your mate what he or she is sorry for. Explain how the mistake affected a deeper condition like respect or trust. Third, coach your mate into coming up with an idea about how he or she can prevent it from happening again. Since you are guiding the conversation, you may have to offer up some ideas. Once you arrive at a plan that satisfies both of you, remind your mate that each time she sticks to that plan, it sends the message that she loves and cares about you.

❤ ❤ ❤

Once you view apologies as conversation problems, not people problems, the hurtful blunders that you or your mate commit will no longer be a sore spot in your relationship. So long as the two of you generally foster goodwill toward each other, the 5-minute apology conversation will help your relationship overcome the obstacles and mistakes that every couple experiences time and again. In fact, every apology will become an opportunity not just to repair your bond, but also to make it stronger.

NEGOTIATE FOR LOVE:
NOTHING IS EVER 50-50

I am not the boss of my house. I don't know how I lost it. I don't know when I lost it. I don't think I ever had it. But I've seen the boss's job and I don't want it.

—BILL COSBY

"I'D DO ANYTHING for her," the husband said to me in marital mediation. His wife glibly responded, "Yeah, sure, he'd do anything for me, except the things I want him to do." When a couple talks like this, it means one thing: They don't know how to negotiate with each other, and their relationship is suffering for it.

Negotiation is the process by which people who want something from each other reach a compromise that determines future behavior. With skillful negotiation, neither partner may be fully satisfied with the result, but they are both better off than they were before. Without good negotiating skills, partners who love each other and would give each other a kidney if necessary find themselves in bitter blowups over little things like taking out the garbage, helping the kids with their homework, doing the grocery shopping, and paying the bills. To make matters worse, these arguments generally increase over time because the division of responsibilities that was acceptable at the start of the relationship becomes obsolete as jobs, family structure, health conditions, and housing situations change over time. What worked before isn't working anymore.

Why is it so hard to shift the burdens of roles and responsibilities? It's because many couples get stuck on their preconceived ideas of what's fair, equal, and acceptable in a love relationship. Sometimes a husband will tell me that since he is the primary breadwinner, his wife should take care of everything in the home, like cooking, cleaning, and raising the kids. Or an exasperated wife will say that since both parents are working, all of the household chores should be split 50-50. Unless by some miracle both partners have exactly the same notion of what's fair (and I have yet to meet a couple for whom that's the case), they will need to meet in the middle somehow.

I Shouldn't Have to Negotiate My Personal Life!

The problem is that negotiation—something we usually think of in the context of the boardroom or courtroom—doesn't feel natural when applied to your personal life. Too many couples refuse to consider negotiation as a tool for keeping their love strong. When I initially discuss the importance of negotiation with a distraught couple, I hear comments like "People negotiate a business deal. I shouldn't have to do that in my personal life," "Why should I negotiate who helps the kids with their homework? I already do so much," and "It's only fair that he should plan dinner at least half the time since we both work. He should know this." Or "Why should I negotiate how I choose to spend my time on Sundays? My wife does whatever she wants during the week and I don't stop her." Each partner wants his or her expectations to be met, but doesn't want to yield anything to meet the mate's expectations.

When we're single, we can believe anything we want about what is fair, but once we're in a relationship, we come up against our partner's notion of fairness. We can get stuck at the boundary with our lists of "what's fair" and "what's nonnegotiable" based on our expectations, the values with which we were raised, or our experiences in past relationships. Or, we can open our minds, reject stereotypes, and keep love alive by finding a unique solution that satisfies both partners.

In this chapter, you'll find out what is truly nonnegotiable and what should be up for discussion. You'll also learn about the four guiding principles of negotiating with someone you love. Lastly, you'll discover how to negotiate for love in 5 minutes or less so your relationship prospers.

TAKE NOTE

Dividing everything 50-50 sounds great in theory, but it's hard for most couples to make it a reality. Instead of getting stuck on making things mathematically equitable, focus on negotiating a balance that works for your lives.

Don't Waste Your Energy: Certain Things Are Nonnegotiable

It's important to distinguish between things that are genuinely nonnegotiable and things that you're just stubborn about. When it comes right down to it, there are very few things that are truly nonnegotiable. What can't be negotiated? Basically, anything you can't control. For example, you can't negotiate someone else's actions, such as "If you would help me more around the house, my

mother would stop interfering and accusing you of being lazy."
You have no control over what your mother or anyone else will do.
You can only control yourself. You also can't negotiate unpredict-
able things like the weather or your health, and you certainly can't
negotiate a past action or behavior. What's done is done, so don't
get trapped by talking about the past. Negotiations deal with the
here and now and the future.

Go for It: What Is Negotiable

What you *can* negotiate is your own future behavior: your words,
actions, and decisions. What you will do and how you will do it,
what you will say, how you will respond, and what you will
decide are all things that can be dealt with at the negotiating
table. This means that while you can't negotiate how you feel
about your partner's friends, for example, you can negotiate
what you will say about them and how much time you are willing
to spend with them.

You may not *want* to negotiate any of these things, but if you
want to fight less and love more, you have to be willing to try. Language like "I have a right to . . . " or "He shouldn't have any say in
how I . . . " has no place in a negotiation. These comments are simply selfish ways of allowing you to remove something that is fair
game from the negotiating table.

Love Negotiations versus Business Negotiations

In a business negotiation your goal is to win by persuading the
other party to give you as much as you can possibly get while giving as little as possible in return. You don't have much concern for
whether or not the business colleague is as satisfied with the outcome as you are. But in a love negotiation, you must never, ever
try to win at all costs. A love negotiation is not a game in which

you aim to score points or exploit your partner's weaknesses for your own advantage. It should be a caring process that leads to a compromise that benefits you both.

In business, you might deliberately negotiate a salary raise while in the midst of an ongoing, intense project because you know your boss's weakness: He can't find a replacement for you at that time, so he'll have to agree to some of your terms. But in a love negotiation, trying to leverage your partner's vulnerability is not to anyone's advantage. For example, if you choose to talk at a time when your partner is so beaten down by work that you know he'll agree to anything to avoid a fight, you may win a petty, short-lived victory, but any plan he agrees to when he's too stressed out to focus is not likely to be one he'll abide by.

The Four Guiding Principles of Love Negotiations

1. Avoid a Pyrrhic Victory

In 280 BC, a Greek king named Pyrrhus of Epirus led his army to victory in a hard-fought war with the Romans. But victory came at a terrible price for the Greeks—King Pyrrhus's army suffered great casualties. When it was over, King Pyrrhus said that one more such victory would undo him.

I use this term to help you understand that in a love relationship, winning at all costs is a terrible thing. Even if you have technically won a battle, doing so at the expense of your mate's needs will plant the seeds of anger and resentment that can undo an entire relationship. The goal of a love negotiation is to find a trade-off of tasks and responsibilities that satisfies both people. Neither you nor your partner should expect to be either ecstatic about or horribly disappointed by the results of a negotiation. Rather, you both should expect to feel satisfied, respected, and, most of all, loved.

2. Tell It Like It Is

In business negotiations, it can be to a person's advantage to mislead, lie, or exaggerate needs or limits. For instance, your boss might tell you, "We can only afford to give you a raise of $3,000 a year because the profit margin of the company won't allow for more." When your boss eventually agrees to a $4,000 raise, you are thrilled. However, the truth was that the boss could have offered you a $6,000 raise without significantly impacting the company's profitability. Misleading statements can sometimes work in business negotiations because each person is trying to get the best deal without concern for the impact it may have on the other.

In love negotiations, the opposite principle applies. Telling each other the complete and total truth about your preferences and what you'd be willing to give up is vital because that's the only way to reach an agreement without anyone feeling shortchanged, bitter, and resentful.

I've found that many of my female clients tend to underplay their needs and limitations in negotiations. This is usually for one of two reasons: They are afraid of upsetting their partner, or they suppress their own needs because they don't want to fulfill the stereotype of the nagging wife.

My Personal Love Negotiation

I had a dilemma in my own life that left me feeling resentful toward my husband. With a young son at home, either my husband or I needed to be in the room with him at any given time to make sure he was safe. In the evenings, when both my husband and I were home, somehow I was always the one who ended up being on surveillance duty. My husband was nearby, but I was "in charge." I would leave the room to make a phone call or use the bathroom or put something away, but I would have a nagging, guilty feeling that I had to hurry back. If we ordered food for dinner, he was eager to go out and pick it up, leaving me at home with our son. As months passed, I realized that I resented my husband for leaving because I wanted to go out and pick up the food so I could have a few minutes of alone time! I wanted to make a phone call and not feel guilty about leaving my husband watching over our son if it lasted more than 2 minutes. I wanted the freedom to occasionally take a hot shower in the evening. But I didn't have those options, and that was a dilemma.

Was the situation of my own doing? The answer is partly yes, partly no. Though my husband never explicitly said it was my job to watch my son in the evenings, he didn't say the opposite, either. But then again, how would he know that I was unhappy with the circumstances if I didn't tell him? Besides, he was happy with the way things were, so why would he want to change anything?

Regardless, it didn't matter to me how we'd gotten to this point. What did matter was that we needed to negotiate our way out of it. So I decided to fess up and put my cards on the table. It wasn't an easy conversation to initiate because I knew that if I became too emotional, I could cross the line into blaming him entirely, and as a result, he'd be likely to get defensive and dig in his heels. So instead, I tried to explain what I needed and why. I wasn't asking him to be "in charge" all the time or even exactly 50 percent of the time, but when he got home from work, I wanted him to offer to play with our son for a half hour to give me some downtime. If we ordered dinner, I wanted to be able to pick it up sometimes so I could have those few minutes to myself. If I needed to make a phone call, I wanted to know I could tell him that I was going to go in the other room and make the call without feeling pressured to rush back. My husband has a lot of wonderful qualities, but mind reading is not one of them. Not surprisingly, after I was assertive about what I needed, we both made changes for the better. My husband began to thoroughly enjoy the focused playtime with our son, and my feelings of resentment evaporated. With both of us in better moods in the evenings, family time became a lot more fun.

3. Get Rid of the Judge and the Jury

Keep Your Mouth Shut

One of the hardest parts of negotiating a deal with your mate is that it's too easy to let people around you get involved and influence you. They might regularly judge what's happening in your relationship and remind you that you aren't getting a "fair" deal. While it's easy for your mother, best friend, or co-worker to tell you that your wife henpecks you for making you do the laundry or that you should go on a "Mom strike" for a week because your husband is taking advantage of you, their opinions have no place in your negotiation. Your friends and family are always going to be prone to siding with you because they want the best for you. But a love negotiation is not about what's right and wrong in the eyes of outsiders; it's about what works best for both members of the couple—and you and your partner are the only people who know what works for you. So be sure to keep your love negotiations behind closed doors. Don't share specific details with others, and let them know that you don't need or want their input on these personal matters.

Don't Make Comparisons

You also want to avoid comparing yourselves to other couples. For instance, if your friend's husband, Jeff, gets up 3 nights a week with the baby and your husband only does it once a week, you might find yourself saying (or thinking) something like "You should be doing what Jeff does." Voicing those thoughts is never a good idea, because you put your mate in the position of defending himself against the charge that he is not as good a partner or father as someone else. Furthermore, comparisons are useless because all people are unique, having different jobs, work hours, personalities, responsibilities, and preferences. You did not marry Jeff, you married your husband, and you have to do what works in *your* relationship. Creating comparisons will only prevent you from seeing what's special and valuable in your own relationship.

4. Know the Alternative

If your 5-minute love negotiation conversation turns into an all-out brawl and you walk away without an agreement, what then? You're not in a business negotiation where you can find another buyer or seller willing to give you a better deal. When a love negotiation falls through, you'll find yourself in a tough situation because there are only two alternatives left: One is to totally give in and remain stressed and angry, while the other is to find a different partner who you think will be more willing to give you what you want. This is where the concept of the best alternative to a negotiated agreement, or BATNA, can be helpful. Coined by Roger Fisher and William Ury of the Harvard Negotiation Project in their book *Getting to Yes,* the term reminds us to be aware of our best alternatives *before* we negotiate. In the case of a love negotiation, if you're becoming angry and are tempted to walk away because you're getting less than you want, consider your two other options. You will see that it's in your best interest to go back to the negotiating table and find a compromise because the reality is that it's better than either alternative. When you return to the negotiating table, try to articulate the reasons for your needs and limits as clearly as you can. It's possible that your mate hasn't fully understood where you're coming from.

The 5-Minute Love Negotiation Conversation

No matter what issue you're confronting, here are the steps to negotiate the best possible outcome for you, your mate, and your relationship.

Step #1: State Your Problem

Explain the problem without placing blame on your mate. How do you do this? Keep your purpose in mind. You are not at the negotiating table to argue about the past, which is unchangeable, but to create a better future. It will be hard for your partner to ignore the problem when you phrase it in a way that doesn't place the blame on him or her. For example, you might say, "I'm completely overwhelmed with the kids and chores. I've tried managing the responsibilities for a while now, and I just can't. I need your help."

Step #2: State Your Mate's Problem

Since this is a love negotiation and you care about finding a solution that works for both of you, this step requires you to define the problem from your mate's perspective. If you show your mate that you understand where he is coming from, he'll be far less likely to mount a defensive response to your requests. Continuing with the prior example, you might say, "I know it's hard for you to think about doing more around the house because you're so busy already, but we've got to find a solution that works for both of us."

Step #3: Make Trade-Offs

Forget about striking a perfect balance. Instead, aim for a solution that works in your relationship based on each other's preferences (perhaps one of you is a morning person and therefore could do some tasks that need to be done in the morning) and skills (maybe the partner who's better at math should be the one to balance the checkbook). Be honest about what you truly need and what you can live without. Ask your mate to do the same and start bartering.

For instance, "Since you really don't like cooking and I absolutely hate cleaning up afterward, can we each do the task we hate the least—I'll cook and you clean?" Or, if you both want to sleep late on the weekend rather than waking up early with the kids, say, "How about if I get up at 6:30 when the baby gets up and you get up at 8:30 and take over while I go back to sleep?" Or, if neither of you wants to cut the grass, "How about if we save money by eating out less and put that money toward hiring a gardener?"

Step #4: Make It Temporary

Make a point of explaining that whatever agreement you come to will always be open for discussion again. The goal is to find what works best for both of you, so if one of you is unhappy with the arrangement a week later, clearly you need to revisit the solution you came up with. You can agree to set the trial period for a week, a month, a weekend, or whatever works for you.

Here's another real-life example of a love negotiation in action.

Step #1: State the Problem

"When we stay at your parents' house for the whole weekend, it doesn't give me any alone time with you, which I enjoy after working all week."

Step #2: State Your Mate's Problem

"I know it's important for us and our children to spend time with your parents and that you want me to enjoy our visits there."

Step #3: Make Trade-Offs

"How about if rather than us staying at your parents' place, which I know you'd prefer, we invite them to stay at our house one weekend? That way we can see them and they can babysit, giving us a little more alone time together."

Step #4: Make It Temporary

"Let's try this for one weekend, and then we can talk about how it went and see if we want to have them over again or visit them the next time."

Is There Anything You'd Be Willing to Do?

No problem can stand the assault of sustained thinking.

—**VOLTAIRE**

If your partner likes things just the way they are and stubbornly refuses to take part in the negotiation, keep thinking and offer new trade-off ideas. Then ask him to chime in with some ideas of his own. If that doesn't work, ask this final question, which is likely to elicit a more positive response: "Is there anything at all that you'd be willing to do?" Putting it in such stark terms will probably eke out some sort of concession from your mate.

When It's Only Words: Noncompliance

No matter how much it appears that you and your mate are both committed to following through on the agreement, there's always a chance that he will conveniently forget a task or refuse to do something after he thinks about it more. Here's what to say to get your mate back on track.

Getting Your Noncompliant Mate to Follow Through

1. Give a reason why you still want your mate to fulfill the agreement.
2. Let your mate save face. Assume that there is a reason why the task wasn't done or the agreement wasn't fulfilled and ask, "I guess there's a reason why you're waiting to do this. Can you tell me what it is?"
3. Ask for a self-imposed deadline when appropriate: "When do you think you'll be able to take care of that?"

♥ ♥ ♥

The result of a good love negotiation is not a perfect outcome, but an outcome in which things are better for you and your partner than they were before the negotiation. I can't emphasize enough how important it is for your expectations to be in line with that reasoning. Avoiding or walking away from a love negotiation because you're reluctant to compromise will only compromise your relationship. At times, you may negotiate an agreement that gives you little of what you originally wanted, but your partnership will be stronger when you and your mate find a solution that addresses both of your needs. It can be hard to stay positive when you know you're agreeing to something that isn't exactly what you would like, but keep the big picture in mind. Remember, too, that in a healthy relationship you must give to get. Perhaps in the next negotiation you will come away with the bigger slice of pie. Each and every time, maintain optimism and remember, you are negotiating with someone with whom you share a bedroom—not the boardroom.

15

CONTROL
OVERREACTIONS:
GET YOUR POINT ACROSS

For every romantic possibility, no matter how robust, there exists at least one equal and opposite sentence, phrase, or word... capable of extinguishing it.

—MALCOLM GLADWELL

OKAY, SO YOU think you're a perfectly reasonable and logical person. But sometimes, when something is said or done that makes you feel criticized, ignored, or disrespected, you shout out your defense and soon find yourself engaged in a full-blown war of words. You know the situation is out of control and going from bad to worse, but you don't know what else to say to get your (totally reasonable!) point across.

What is an overreaction, in the context of a relationship? It's when you passionately react to a situation that disturbs you without clearly expressing the reasons for your overblown response.

Even if the storm of overreaction passes quickly, the hangover leaves its mark. Your partner remains unsure of exactly what he or she did to provoke such a dramatic response, while you continue to fume over your mate's offense.

Adding Fuel to the Fire

Many overreaction scenarios follow a familiar path, with a few innocent statements suddenly escalating into all-out battle.

"Can I use the computer now?" is a simple request.

"I'm busy. Soon" is a simple response.

"Soon? Just get off that stupid computer already. You're always on it!"

"You're overreacting! Who says I have to do everything you want the second you ask?"

If anything intensifies an overreaction, it's being told by someone that you are overreacting. When we're confronted with this response, we have a choice: We can blame our mate for making us overreact, or we can reconsider our role in creating this situation.

This can be really hard to do. I'm sure you think your emotional response is warranted because your mate is being unaccommodating, overly critical, or rude. Perhaps your mate has done this often, and you've reached your limit. Whatever the situation, the reality is that overreacting is never acceptable. All it does is heighten anger and resentment, causing retaliation.

From Bad to Worse

Our response to our partner's imperfections can either encourage a flaw or help to make it better. For instance, a friend of mine was playing with her 4-year-old daughter in her bedroom while her husband was watching TV in the living room. My friend was having a nice time playing with her 4-year-old daughter until suddenly she looked up and saw her husband in the doorway, shutting the bedroom door without saying a word. Annoyed, she got up, pushed the door open, walked straight to the living room, and yelled loudly enough for her daughter to hear, "You are so rude!" Her husband replied, "Well, I didn't want to hear all the noise you two were making with Emma's toy piano." "Noise?" she countered. "The sound of your daughter playing is noise to you? If you were a good father you'd shut off the TV right now and come play with us."

My friend's anger is understandable, but yelling at her husband over such a small thing, and within earshot of her daughter? That's inappropriate. And connecting his shutting the door to the notion that he's a bad father? Overreaction. Do you think her husband came in to play with his daughter after that hot verbal exchange? No. He tuned out and kept watching TV.

Tantrums Are Reserved for Children

Simply put, overreacting is an adult temper tantrum, and it's a terrible way to get what you want. Changing your mate's undesirable qualities or habits won't happen through threats or name-calling. It doesn't happen when you're assuming, misjudging, and implying that your mate is to blame for any and all of what went wrong that day, that week, or that year. Change happens when you intentionally and rationally say the right words at the right time to achieve mutual understanding.

A Gap That Must Be Filled

Overreactions usually happen when there's a gap between how we feel and what we say. In the example of the door-shutting incident, my friend didn't explain to her husband that she felt like their daughter was missing out on special father-daughter time. She wasn't really upset about the door, but rather about the fact that even on the weekends when her husband was home, she was still saddled with the full-time responsibility of finding activities to occupy their daughter. She was frustrated because she felt that her husband used watching TV to escape from spending time with the family, and she would have loved to have some escape time herself. All of these points are reasonable, but they weren't articulated in the heat of the moment. If my friend really wanted to confront the issue of family time, she needed to sit down with her husband later that day and fill in the gaps between what she said and what she meant.

When we don't fully explain ourselves, we leave the door open for an overreaction that breeds anger, resentment, and antagonism. By learning how to effectively close the gap between what we're thinking and what we're saying, we can prevent conflict.

This chapter will help you determine whether or not you are an overreactor; if you are, you'll learn how easy it is to get rid of that label. If it's your mate who's the overreactor, you'll learn what to say to turn down the heat by turning up the logic. Take this quiz to find out where you stand.

Quiz: Are You an Overreactor?

Select your most likely response to these five situations.

1. After you get into a tiff with your sister, your mate tells you, "You could have handled that better." You say:
   A. "I guess so."
   B. "I'd like to see you try to handle it better!"
   C. "What do you mean?"

2. Your mate says, "I told our neighbors that they can use our driveway to park their car when we're on vacation. I hope that doesn't bother you." You say:

    A. "Okay, whatever."

    B. "How could you do that without asking me first?"

    C. "It does bother me a little. If they're not around when we get home, we won't be able to pull our car up to the house to unload all of our stuff."

3. You're meeting your partner at a restaurant for dinner, but she arrives an hour late. When she apologizes, you say:

    A. "That's okay."

    B. "You should be sorry! Do you think I have nothing better to do than sit here and wait for you?"

    C. "I wish you had called. If I'd known you wouldn't be ready for another hour, I would have stayed at work later and finished my project."

4. Friends of yours are dropping by soon, but when you ask your mate to clean up the living room, he says, "Sure, as soon as this TV show is over." You say:

    A. "Fine, I'll clean it up now."

    B. "I can't believe you're watching TV. I ask you for one thing and you won't even do that."

    C. "Our friends could be here any minute, and I have to get the food ready. Can you clean up the living room while you're watching your show?"

5. Your partner tells you that she wants to invite your least favorite neighbors to a barbecue you're hosting at your home. You say:

    A. "Okay, if you want to."

B. "Why would you do that? I hate those people!"

C. "I'd rather not because we've had them over to our house three times this year and they've never reciprocated."

Results

If you chose mostly As, you are:

The Underreactor

It's impossible for me to believe that you wouldn't be bothered by any of these scenarios. With your totally passive attitude, you're taking the easy way out of confrontation by giving in and turning yourself into a human doormat. Could it be that you underreact because you don't want to be labeled demanding or nagging? That's understandable, but when you don't react, your mate may interpret your nonreaction as, at best, a sign of weakness or indifference or, at worst, an indication of a lack of love. In fact, your lack of reaction may tempt your partner to overreact just to get a rise out of you.

If you chose mostly Bs, you are:

The Overreactor

Your first instinct is to come at your partner full blast, trying to force him or her to do what you want, when you want it. Ironically, the more you overreact, the less your partner will listen to you. Yes, there may be legitimate reasons why you feel the way you do, but even when your overreaction feels justified, it's not, because it will only lead to conflict. Once you understand why you overreact, you will be able to turn down your aggressive force and become a smart reactor who speaks with tact and respect.

If you chose mostly Cs, you are:

The Smart Reactor

You are assertive, meaning that you make your thoughts known without stepping on your partner's toes. You recognize that your partner does not have the right to insist that you agree with him or her all the time, and yet you don't disagree without a good reason. You are aware of your thoughts, and you express them. You ask relevant questions and share your reasoning to make yourself understood.

The more As or Bs you chose, the more likely it is that your relationship is headed for a collision. It's time to change your words to change your relationship.

What's the Matter with You?!

People who overreact often do so because they typecast their mate with certain negative traits. When you don't take the time to either understand your partner or make yourself understood, you jump to conclusions about his or her motives. He's lazy. She's inconsiderate. He's self-centered. Because you view your partner's actions through the lens of this perceived flaw, you assume the worst and react accordingly. The result: a dramatic outburst that leaves your mate confused—and possibly questioning your sanity. Here are a few examples:

Example #1: "You're So Uncooperative!"

You know this one.

"Honey, can you take out the garbage now?" you say to your mate.

"I'll do it later."

"I am asking you to do it now. Can't you just do it?"

"I said I would. Stop making such a big deal out of it."

"I am not asking you to take the garbage all the way to the dump. I'm asking you to walk 20 steps to the edge of the driveway. Why are you being so difficult?"

"If it's so easy, why don't you do it yourself?"

And then the big fight begins.

Reality Check: Find the Gap

What's the gap in this situation that's causing such confusion and anger? It's that one partner doesn't understand why "now" is so important, and the other partner assumes his or her mate is deliberately being difficult.

Perhaps the "perfect" mate would obediently jump up and take out the garbage at the first request. But no one is perfect, so we must have reasonable expectations. It's unreasonable to expect that someone will do, think, or say something just because he or she is directed to.

You may have had any number of logical reasons for wanting your mate to take out the garbage now instead of later, but you didn't voice them. Maybe the dog discovered the smell of chicken remnants in the garbage and was about to tear open the bag, or perhaps the trash can was nearly overflowing and you needed to throw something away, or maybe it was 7:00 in the morning and the garbage truck would be arriving at any minute.

Because you didn't express the reason for the urgency of the situation—and because you didn't stop to ask about your mate's reason for wanting to wait—you assumed that your partner was just being stubborn. The gap between what each of you was thinking and what was expressed allowed conflict to seep in.

Generally speaking, we do have reasons for wanting things to be done, but we must express those reasons. We cannot expect our mate to read our mind. If, however, you don't have a clear reason for wanting something done immediately, then you have to accept that the task isn't time sensitive and you need to either let your partner do it on his or her own timetable or do it yourself. By not insisting that everything be done when you demand, you show your partner that you value his or her time, and your requests will be taken more seriously.

TAKE NOTE

If something is not time sensitive, don't ask for it to be done immediately. Instead, ask, "When do you think you'll be able to do it?"

Example #2: "You're So Irresponsible!"

If you believe your mate always overspends, you might call up this belief when she happens to suggest that she wants to move to a bigger home. You may even go nuts, yelling, "You always want things we can't afford. Can't you do math? We can't pay for a house like that unless one of us gets a major raise."

Reality Check: Find the Gap

If you asked a question as simple as "Why?" before reacting, you might find out that your partner would like to move to a bigger place—but one that's in a less expensive neighborhood or closer to her parents so you could get more free babysitting help. These are logical reasons for a move, and both are things that would actually help save money. Here, the gap between thoughts and words resulted from a presumption about a flaw.

We all have triggers that can lead us to make incorrect conclusions and shut down our ability to listen. But even if your mate does have a tendency to spend too much money, it's important that you don't view everything through the prism of that trait. If she did in fact want to move to a more expensive place, then you should ask her to explain how she expected the family to afford it. In the TV series *Mad Men,* the main character, Don Draper, a successful advertising man, had a great line we can all take to heart: "If you don't like what is being said, then change the conversation." If you want to talk about family finances, then bring out the bank statements and the calculator; don't keep talking about moving to another house.

TAKE NOTE

When your partner says something that doesn't sound right to you, don't assume the worst. Put on your detective hat and ask questions to find out more information.

Example #3: "You Don't Care about Me!"

I've heard variations on this dozens of times in mediation. One married couple, Steve and Margo, told me about their most recent episode of overreaction.

"We went to the movies with my friend Mike and his new girlfriend last night," Steve told me. "It was a romantic comedy, and the main characters were a married couple who had big problems getting along."

Margo then jumped in and continued, "After the movie Mike made a nasty comment comparing me to the lead female character in the movie. He said, 'That wife in the movie reminds me of you, Margo. The couple's troubles boiled down to one thing: The wife wears the pants in the relationship.' I couldn't believe he said that!"

"Then what happened?" I asked.

Margo said, "I got angry and told Mike that he was wrong

about the comparison. He tried to defend himself by saying he was just kidding, but I knew he wasn't."

Steve continued telling me the story. "The whole thing should have ended right there, but of course Margo wouldn't let it go. When we got home afterward and we were alone, she went ballistic, accusing Mike of horrible things and then yelling at me for being friends with him. She told me she'd never go out with Mike again." Then Steve turned to his wife: "You know you totally overreacted, as usual. I mean, Mike shouldn't have compared you to the wife in the movie, but it was only a movie, and he said he was kidding. You talk like Mike is the devil."

"I wasn't overreacting!" Margo exclaimed. "Mike compared me to a crazy woman. Don't you get it? I wouldn't be surprised if Mike got that idea from you!"

"Now you've flipped out," Steve shot back. "He didn't call you crazy. You're making things up. Don't blame me because you read into everything!"

I stopped their pointless argument and tried to help Margo fill in the gap between what she was thinking and what she was saying.

"Margo, it's clear that you were insulted by Mike's comment. But you are aware that your husband can't control what Mike says. So why are you so mad at your husband?"

Margo answered, "Because Steve should have told Mike that he was wrong! But he kept his mouth shut."

"So are you upset with your husband because he didn't defend you?"

"Yes. He did the same thing he always does when there is a problem—he keeps quiet."

I asked her, "What did it mean to you when your husband didn't react to Mike's comment?"

"That's easy," she answered. "It meant he agreed with him."

I turned to Steve. "Did you agree with Mike?"

"No, I didn't."

"Then why didn't you defend me?" Margo asked.

Steve answered, "Look, we were all having a good time, so I didn't want to start a fight. Besides, I've known Mike for years, and everyone knows you can't take him seriously. He's never been married, and trust me, it's for a very good reason."

I probed further. "So by avoiding a problem with your friend, you caused one with your wife?"

That question got Steve thinking. "I guess I did," he admitted. "But at the time, I didn't see it that way."

Reality Check: Find the Gap

After this discussion, Steve recognized that when he underreacts, he causes waves in his relationship. In the mediation, he committed to becoming a more active participant in these scenarios and defending his wife when someone insults her, joke or no joke (see Chapter 6 for more about why you *must* always defend your mate to others).

Then I talked with Margo about how she could learn to stop overreacting in the future. She finally understood that what bothered her was not the friend's comment; rather, it was what she perceived as her husband's passivity and nonreactive behavior. That was the gap between what she was thinking and what she was saying.

Now that she knew how to identify moments when her husband didn't react, she could replace an overreaction episode in which she blamed him for everything with a calmer conversation specifically about why he stayed silent and how that affected her.

Pay attention to situations when your mate doesn't react. Later, ask him or her why it happened and explain how it made you feel.

The 5-Minute Anti-Overreaction Conversation

The next time a situation occurs in which you typecast your mate with a negative trait, stop, count slowly to 10, and then begin this 5-minute anti-overreaction conversation.

Step #1: Clarify with Questions

Make sure you didn't misjudge what your partner said. Say, "I want to understand what you're thinking." Ask clarifying questions like "Why do you want to do it later and not now?" or "How come you didn't respond when he said that?" or "Do you think we can afford to get a bigger place?"

Assume you do not know the answers to these questions. Listen closely and you will discover that the person might have a very legitimate reason for saying what he said or acting the way she did.

Step #2: Reason with Explanations

Reason with your mate. Come up with one or two reasons to explain what you are thinking. Think hard and make sure your reasons are logical before you speak. Also, if you are upset with your mate, make sure it's because of something that is within your mate's control. For example, in the case of Steve and Margo, Steve was not in control of Mike's comment, but he did have control over his reaction to it.

Step #3: Check In for Agreement

This step requires you to bite your lip and let go of a little pride. Check in with your mate by asking this question: "Does what I'm saying make any sense to you?" If your reasons are legitimate and you're presenting them clearly, your mate will hopefully answer yes. If your mate says no, you might need to offer a different reason or try to be less emotional in your argument. Or, there's always the chance that your mate simply doesn't agree with your perspective. Listen to him or her; you might discover that your partner has some valid points that you hadn't thought of that might change your mind. Also consider the option of overlooking the incident if your mate's reasoning makes sense and the incident has no lasting harmful effect on you.

"But What If My Mate Overreacts?"

Let's not forget about the other side of the coin. What if your mate criticizes you or misjudges something you said or did by viewing it through the lens of a flaw he believes you have? Your first thought might be "There he goes again, accusing me of being irresponsible!"

Now that you know the 5-minute anti-overreaction conversation, you can simply turn it around anytime you feel your mate may be overreacting. You have to assume that there is a gap between what he is thinking and feeling and what is being communicated to you. Simply say, "I think you're jumping to conclusions. Let me explain myself better." Change the tone of the conversation with calm, wise words.

♥ ♥ ♥

As a mediator it is my job to identify the gaps and help couples close them. Although I can't physically be by your side as you do this for yourself, you will have a mediator with you in spirit. As you go through the 5 minute conversation, stay calm and focused and remind yourself that you are basically mediating your own dispute. Both an underreactor and an overreactor contribute to a cycle of disagreement and hostility between partners, whereas a smart reactor creates a cycle of tolerance and understanding. Use the skills of a mediator and you can confidently walk away from a conversation knowing that you meant what you said and said what you meant.

16

DISARM THE KNOW-IT-ALL: REGAIN CONFIDENCE IN EACH OTHER

I married Miss Right. I just didn't know her first name was Always.

—HENNY YOUNGMAN

AH, THE KNOW-IT-ALL. He thinks he impresses others with his bountiful intelligence and vast knowledge. And yet it doesn't take long before the people around him start to suspect that he actually knows only a fraction of the things he claims to know. In fact, you might even begin to think that when it comes to certain topics, he really knows nothing at all.

Not everyone has a know-it-all in his or her life—but if someone you love is a know-it-all, I'll bet you're nodding your head in recognition right now. Let's admit that know-it-alls mean no harm and, usually, their actions don't hurt anyone. The problem is that when one partner constantly claims to know things he doesn't really know, it becomes impossible for his mate to believe anything he says. The mate of a know-it-all might feel the need to check all information that comes from the partner because history has proven that when the know-it-all's statements are accepted as truth, mistakes are often made. Result: some serious relationship blowups.

It's Not Funny: Christina and Eric's Story

"Tell your friend Joe to make an appointment with Dr. Tom Whyte. Tom is one of the best ear, nose, and throat doctors in the area," Christina says to her husband, Eric.

"Really? How do you know that?" asks Eric.

"Well, whenever I see his wife at school, she tells me stories about his patients and how they absolutely love him. Tom even has some celebrity clients, so he must be one of the best in his field."

"Christina, the few times I met him he seemed like a nice guy, but being nice and having some celebrity clients doesn't make him one of the best doctors in the city."

"Trust me, Eric. I know what I'm talking about. I would definitely go to Tom if I needed an ENT specialist."

"Tom might be a good doctor, but come on, Christina, you've never met any of his patients. Do you really think his wife would tell you if any of them were unhappy with his care?"

"Why do you always doubt me? Do you think I'm an idiot? It's not funny. It's as if you're programmed to disagree with whatever I say."

"Maybe that's because you don't know what you're talking about. Do you know where Tom went to school? Where was he trained? How long has he been in private practice? Have you looked at the reports on the best doctors?"

"Why are you putting me on the witness stand? You're so condescending."

"I don't think it's condescending to ask you how you know something. You make things up and come to conclusions without information."

"So now I make things up? Why do I even bother talking to you? All you do is judge everything I say."

Why Don't You Trust Me?

Many couples get caught up in fights like Eric and Christina's. These frustrating disagreements usually come down to one question: "Why don't you believe what I say?" Ironically, the other person has answered that question repeatedly: "I don't believe you because you often say things without facts to back them up." The know-it-all doesn't like this answer, so she responds by defending her original statements. Round and round it goes, each time ending with the same explosion.

If Christina could take a step back and read the transcript of this disagreement, she might be able to see that her assessment of Dr. Whyte was based on anecdotal evidence. People mistrust others who express strong opinions without having facts to back them up. At times, these types of misleading statements can even be seen as a form of lying or trying to hide the truth. People dislike being misled so much that they relish the opportunity to prove a know-it-all wrong—even when that person is their mate.

Ripple Effects of the Know-It-All Habit

Arrogance

Misleading or speaking as if one's opinion is fact is unacceptable, but to make matters worse, this know-it-all communication habit is usually accompanied by an arrogant attitude: "How dare you question me?" The know-it-all hates being questioned because it uncovers his exaggerations, gullibility, and lack of facts, which makes him feel inferior, insecure, and unknowledgeable. He automatically defends himself, which leads to disagreements, intolerance, and lasting resentment.

The Double-Check Habit

Recently I heard this complaint from a client: "My wife asked me how far a certain restaurant is from our friend's house. I told her it was only minutes away, and then I caught her on the computer checking up on my answer. It made me furious. Why should I bother to answer her questions if she's not going to trust what I say and she'll double-check my answer?" When I delved further into this double-checking behavior, his wife said that she didn't want to have to double-check the information her husband offered, but when something affected her (like what time they needed to pick up their friends to make sure they wouldn't be late for a dinner reservation), she felt she had to double-check because her husband had often been wrong.

This particular woman, like any other person who is in a relationship with a know-it-all, gradually lost confidence or trust that the information given by the know-it-all was accurate, so she felt compelled to double-check her partner's assertions, pushing his anger button and compounding the problem.

One-Upmanship

Sometimes a know-it-all's need to impress others leads him to contradict or one-up his partner in public. It's important that you address this immediately. Privately explain to your partner that although his additional information might be accurate, you feel humiliated when he tells others that you are wrong. Ask him not to correct you in public unless his information is relevant to an immediate decision or emergency.

Not every couple suffers from know-it-all-it is, but if your relationship has any of the signs, this chapter will serve as your wake-up call. For some of us, this habit has been going on for decades, yet we're barely aware of the friction it causes. Whether your partner is a know-it-all or you're honest enough to recognize the know it all symptoms in yourself, it's important to identify this trait so you can eliminate its negative effects on your relationship.

Why Do Know-It-Alls Act as if They Know It All?

There's nothing inherently evil about stretching the truth or making up bits and pieces of information to make a point. A know-it-all doesn't set out to harm people. Most often, she simply wants to engage in a conversation in which she looks smart and confident. Know-it-all tendencies can even sometimes be charming, when the know-it-all's extreme statements and expressions of certainty add to the excitement of a conversation in a social situation. But this same tendency can turn poisonous when displayed on the home front with a mate.

Here are some of the reasons why know-it-alls exaggerate and mislead.

1. They want to sound intelligent but haven't taken the time to learn the facts.
2. They want to make a powerful point, so they embellish what they're saying for added impact.
3. They want something to be true, so they talk as if it were true.
4. They want to display self-confidence through certainty. (In fact, many know-it-alls are deeply insecure.)
5. They believe what they are saying is accurate because they aren't well enough informed to know what facts are missing.

The Know-It-Alls Who Know Nothing

The only things worth learning are the things you learn after you know it all.
—HARRY S. TRUMAN

Telltale Signs: Opinion versus Fact

Underlying the know-it-all habit is a reluctance to acknowledge the difference between an opinion and a fact. For example, "It costs $29.99" is a fact, but "It doesn't cost a lot" is an opinion. "I spoke to our neighbor and that's what they did" is a fact, while "That's the best way to do it" is an opinion. Instead of building an argument out of facts, know-it-alls spin a web of opinions that quickly disintegrates under scrutiny.

Because they secretly know their assertions are built on fragile foundations, know-it-alls tend to cover up their lack of facts in three key ways, which may overlap with one another.

1. **I'm the Expert:** A know-it-all often pretends to have
    expertise in something, whether it's how to build a new
    cabinet, the best driving route to a restaurant, or the
    perfect way to handle a tricky situation. On any given
    day, he could be a food expert, car expert, electronics
    expert, or business expert. This know-it-all may make
    statements like:

    "I've done that a hundred times. I know what to do."
    "I know how to get there. I don't have to ask anyone for
        directions."
    "This is definitely how it's done."

2. **It's My Way or the Highway:** A know-it-all presumes
    that he or she has reached the smartest and best
    conclusion and therefore no other conclusion is
    reasonable, possible, or acceptable. This "I'm right and
    you're wrong" attitude dominates his language:

    "What you're saying doesn't make any sense."
    "You don't know what you're talking about!"
    "There's no better way to do this."
    "You've got it all wrong. Let me tell you how this works."

3. **Because I Said So:** A know-it-all arrives at a decision or
    conclusion without information to back it up. He defends
    his conclusion by using his own certainty as an
    explanation. He might say:

"Trust me, I know what I'm talking about."

"I'm sure that's how it is."

"I have experience here. You don't."

Are You Dumb or Something?

Sarah tells her husband, Brian, that they need to get their driveway repaved because the potholes have gotten so bad she finds herself driving up the side of the driveway just to avoid them.

"Yes, we do need to take care of that," he agrees. "We should use the guys the Solomons just used for their driveway. They were happy with the work, and I'm sure they got the best price."

"When did they have their driveway paved?" asks Sarah.

"Recently."

"How recently? I mean, prices do change."

"I said recently. You know what that means."

"No, I don't. Tell me."

"Wow, you're annoying. Probably a couple months ago."

"Well, I'll have to check on that. But anyway, how do you know they got the best price?"

"Because they're smart people and they spend their money wisely."

"But that doesn't mean they absolutely got the best price. I don't know how good they are at negotiating."

"I'm sure they're as good as you are at negotiating."

"How do you know that?"

"Because I know them!"

"Are you saying I should completely trust who they used and go with that company without personally checking on them or looking into others?"

"Well, go ahead. Do whatever you want. You'll be wasting your time."

Decoding the Argument

In this exchange, Sarah is left justifiably frustrated, resentful, and angry with her husband, who seems to be preventing her from doing her best to make the right decision. And Brian, in turn, feels as though his wife, who wanted his opinion, has now put him through an interrogation.

If Brian's know-it-all habits don't seem obvious to you, here's a breakdown of where he went wrong.

Know-It-All Statement #1: "It Was Recently."

Brian said the Solomons got their driveway repaved recently, even though he didn't know the exact date. Prices change over time, so if he was off by a few months, that could matter. It was misleading to say "recently" when he wasn't sure of when it actually happened. Brian presented his conclusion when he didn't have the facts.

Know-It-All Statement #2: "I'm Sure They Got the Best Price."

Brian assumed that he and Sarah could trust the Solomons to get the best price. If Brian had information about how many driveway companies the Solomons called for quotes, or if he was with them during the negotiating, only then could he vouch for their ability to find the best price. His assumption is based only on his perception that they spend their money wisely (but how could he possibly know the details of their personal finances?). Brian presents information as fact when it's really just his opinion based on shaky assumptions.

Know-It-All Statement #3: "Do Whatever You Want. You'll Be Wasting Your Time."

With this comment, Brian digs in his heels. He turns the tables on his mate in an attempt to make her feel stupid or guilty for taking the time to get more information. He cannot accept that perhaps there could be an advantage to finding out more information.

What If You're the Know-It-All?

If you're the one who thinks you know everything, you should expect certain consequences.

1. **Expect to Be Put on the Witness Stand:** The partner of a know-it-all is constantly in interrogation mode, trying to gather the facts to figure out how the know-it-all came to his or her conclusion. If you're the know-it-all, you'll feel as if you are on the witness stand facing a tough prosecutor.

2. **Expect to Get Angry:** Your partner is going to question your opinions. You're going to get angry when those questions indicate a lack of confidence in your conclusions.

3. **Expect Your Partner to Get Angry with You:** Your partner is going to be turned off by your misleading statements and exaggerations, as well as by your defensive attitude. Your mate is also going to feel disrespected and hurt when you one-up her in public by insinuating that you know more than she does.

4. **Expect a No-Win Result:** You and your partner will lose confidence in and respect for one another.

Eventually, your partner will always suspect that you don't know what you're talking about, even when you do.

Verbal Self-Defense

If you've realized that you're occasionally put on the witness stand for your know-it-all tendencies, that's actually great news. With this new awareness, you can prevent yourself from creating a trust vacuum in your relationship. The next time you find yourself being questioned about the facts, let that be your red flag that you might need to change your approach and words. Use one of these comments to get yourself out of this no-win situation: "I don't have all the facts, but here's what I do know," "I'm not sure, but," "You're right, I haven't looked that up," "I didn't have much time, so I only checked this part," or "With more information, we probably would have a better answer."

The 5-Minute Conversation: Disarming a Know-It-All

If your partner is the one with the problem, this 5-minute conversation is your road map to fixing it. Remember, every person, including the know-it-all, is entitled to her own opinion. There's no need to persuade the know it all to change her opinion to agree with you. The goal of this conversation is to persuade her to understand and acknowledge that what she is stating *is* an opinion, not a fact, and that in certain situations you need more facts.

It's critical that you have this 5-minute conversation the moment that the know-it-all behavior surfaces. Do not wait, because both of you will forget the exact words exchanged, and it will be hard to pin down whether your mate was talking about a fact or an opinion. Open up a conversation like this:

Step #1: Test the Waters

"I know you're sure of what you're saying, but I need some backup facts to be sure I understand where you're coming from." If your partner shares more facts and answers your questions without becoming agitated, then you don't have a problem. But if she becomes defensive and resorts to the "How dare you question me?" attitude, move to Step 2.

Step #2: Identify Opinions versus Facts

"Would you agree that what you just said is your opinion, not a fact? It's your conclusion based on what you believe, isn't it?" Wait for an answer and keep talking about the difference between fact and opinion until your mate gets it. Then say, "I think I'm entitled to have the facts so I can come to my own conclusion. Do you agree?"

Step #3: Get Specific

"Your opinion may be right, but in this case I need to know the answers to X, Y, and Z before I can come to a conclusion. Will you help me find the answers? Can you call ___? Can we find ___, or should I?"

Step #4: Set Expectations

"Sometimes we get stuck arguing because one of us presents an opinion as a fact. In the future, I'm going to be aware of those moments, and when that happens, I will stop our conversation to ask the question 'Is this a fact or your opinion?' If I do that, please don't get angry with me; understand that I'm just trying to get more information so we can have a better outcome. Can we work on this together?"

Creating the Turning Point

Because most know-it-alls don't have bad intentions, your know-it-all partner will probably be willing to admit, when gently pushed, that she is talking about her opinion, not a fact. The habit will almost certainly resurface during another talk, but when you calmly and kindly ask your question—"Is that a fact or your opinion?"—your partner will realize that she's doing it again and both of you will calm down, join forces, and possibly share a knowing smile. That's the turning point. All couples have their glitches. Luckily, if this is one of yours, it isn't one that will make or break your relationship. Together, you can overcome it.

HAVE A
GOOD FIGHT:
END YOUR
BAD FIGHT HABIT

Nothing can keep an argument going like two persons who aren't sure what they're arguing about.

—O. A. BATTISTA

Dear Laurie,

My husband and I have been together for 6 years and we still fight constantly. We fight about stupid stuff, important stuff—you name it, we fight about it. We are still in love and want to be together, but the fighting is really frustrating for both of us and we never seem to settle anything. It's starting to affect every part of our relationship. How can we make it stop?

—Maryanne

How can we stop the fighting? It's the million-dollar question, but it's the wrong question. The right question is: How can we turn our bad fights into good fights? Disagreements are going to happen no matter how great your relationship is, but there are right and wrong ways to handle them. Bad fights, which are loaded with emotional defensive maneuvers and character assassinations, camouflage the actual problem so there's no way to reach a solution. Good fights, which are rational encounters that effectively address the problem at hand, are the route to a peaceful solution. Sometimes your partner will start the fight, and other times it will be you in your attempt to assertively address something that bothers you. Either way, it's your job to guide the disagreement toward a good fight. For some of my mediation clients, bad fighting had become their only way of communicating. They didn't realize that better options were even possible.

HAVE YOU HEARD?

Nearly 70 percent of conflicts between married couples are left unresolved.

So how do you turn a bad fight into a good fight? The answer is the 5-minute anticonflict conversation, a one-size-fits-all formula for peace. The conversation is based on a mediation technique that uses standard steps to identify and isolate the problem at hand so you can reach a solution. Learn the technique now and you can use it to successfully manage any difficult issue that you and your partner face down the road.

The Two Types of Bad Fights

Before we learn this technique and the related 5-minute conversation, let's talk about when it's necessary. I'm sure you've experienced, as most couples have, two of the most common types of bad fights. One of them I call the snowball fight, wherein one or both spouses unknowingly add more and more unrelated topics to a conflict, forcing it to grow bigger with no resolution in sight. The second type is what I call the revolving door fight. Here, the couple continue to revisit a fight or issue they've had before, circling around and around until one partner tires of fighting and simply gives in. Some people are so caught up in the cycle of arguing that they combine both types of fights into one all-encompassing battle.

Rob and Michelle: Married to the Enemy

Married for 9 years, Rob and Michelle spent a year in marital counseling to resolve conflicts about child care and financial issues. As soon as those issues were resolved, different battle topics emerged. On the brink of divorce, they were referred to me for couples mediation. Their real problem, I discovered, wasn't what they disagreed about, but rather their method of arguing. "She's always bringing up the past," complained Rob. "Whenever I mess up, she's sure to remember all the previous times I did something like it and remind me about those mistakes. She goes on and on like a broken record. How could anyone be expected to live with this?"

Not only did this couple engage in bad revolving door fights that kept them stuck in the past, their arguments also snowballed into disagreements about whose behavior was more blameworthy. Michelle complained, "When I try to offer him some criticism, he gets angry, defends himself, and then runs away, slamming the door behind him. If he would just stop getting so defensive and man up to admit his mistakes, I wouldn't get so mad." Michelle was hoping for a reaction she was never going to get. What person isn't going to defend himself when a laundry list of his mistakes and flaws is thrown at him? For his part, Rob was intent on painting his wife as an overbearing woman, even if it meant further antagonizing her. They each saw the other as an enemy who needed to be conquered. There was no way this couple could reach a peaceful agreement on anything, even something as simple as who should take out the garbage.

Stupid Is as Stupid Says

What were Rob and Michelle thinking? Well, the truth is that during their fights, they weren't thinking at all. Their emotional, blame-game reactions overwhelmed their thinking, shutting down the logical part of their brains and rendering them temporarily insane. As a result, they kept saying and doing things that backfired and moved them further away from a solution—and each other.

For many of us, the anger and blaming that an argument ignites, reinforced with bad fight tactics, triggers a fight-or-flight response. Evolutionarily speaking, the fight-or-flight response—the chemical reaction that takes place in our bodies in response to a stressful or threatening situation, elevating levels of stress hormones like adrenaline and causing rapid breathing and heartbeat—aided our species' survival. By short-circuiting the logical mind, these stress hormones enable us to react more swiftly, snapping us into automatic attack-or-flee mode when we're faced with an urgent threat like a roaring saber-toothed tiger or a midnight raid by a neighboring tribe. But in modern relationships, this instinctual response can be harmful. We perceive everything and everyone, including our mate, as the enemy. As a result, our response is not proportional to the trigger—e.g., reacting with road rage when someone cuts us off on the freeway, talking back to our boss when we are criticized, or screaming at our mate who refuses to ask for directions.

Unaware that their brains were being hijacked by their emotions, Rob and Michelle held little hope that they could improve their relationship. Once they understood that they had the power to change their situation, they agreed to make an effort to start replacing their "bad" fights with "good" fights. They used the following checklist to make positive changes that helped them change for the better.

Check Yourself: Are You Having a Fight-or-Flight Response?

Physical Signs

- ✓ Is my heart rate quickening?
- ✓ Am I starting to sweat?
- ✓ Is my breathing rapid and shallow, as if I might hyperventilate?
- ✓ Am I tightening my muscles, frowning, clenching my hands and jaw, or grinding my teeth?

Emotional Signs

- ✓ Do I feel an unstoppable urge to defend myself and prove that my partner is wrong?
- ✓ Is my mind running around in a circle, repeating the same point over and over again?
- ✓ Am I compiling a mental list of my mate's mistakes or flaws?
- ✓ Do I want to just run away because I sense that saying anything else will be useless or even harmful?

If your answer is yes to two or more of these questions, then you are in the midst of a fight-or-flight emotional response. The good news is that as soon as you become conscious of your physical response and the situation, you can turn on your brain with rational thought, counteracting the instinctive (and unproductive) emotional response.

The 5-Minute Anticonflict Conversation: Transforming a Bad Fight into a Good Fight

Step #1: Do Something Different

To use this technique, you must be in a logical state of mind, capable of maintaining self-control. How do you wrestle back control over your emotions? It's simple: You do something different. In his book *Do One Thing Different,* author Bill O'Hanlon shares the example of a couple who were told that when a fight got out of control, they should pause while the husband took off all of his clothes and lay naked in the empty bathtub. The wife should sit on the toilet fully dressed, and then they should continue the fight where they left off. As you can imagine, it was difficult to have an argument that way.

Now, I'm not going to ask you to strip off your clothes (though you should feel free to try it!), but you can do something else to regain control: When you first detect that you are in high anger mode, gather your thoughts and say to your partner, "I'd like to have a 5-minute conversation." Then, before you say or do anything else, sit down wherever you are (the floor is always an option). Ask your mate to sit down as well and face you. It's harder to get yourself in a huff when you are seated and unable to chase your partner around as you scream about your grievances. (If you are out with your mate in public, then hold your tongue until you are together in private.) You'll also short-circuit your fight-or-flight response: While standing keeps your body tensed and ready for action, sitting sends a signal to your brain that you won't be wrestling any lions or fleeing for the hills right now. Doing this one thing differently gets you out of the routine of your fighting habit and opens the door to a new, rational way to handle the situation.

Step #2: Be a Detective

When we are stuck in an emotional fight, we impulsively make assumptions about our partner's intentions. But if those assumptions are wrong, as they often are, we end up getting sidetracked into a different battle, leaving the real problem unsolved. If you're going to have a rational good fight, then you have to reject assumptions and go straight for the facts. You do this by being a detective and asking neutral questions.

When you ask neutral questions like those listed below, not only will you uncover intent and discover the real problem, you will also show respect for your mate's point of view. Remember, respect is an essential condition for love.

Examples of Neutral Questions

"Why do you think that?"
"What makes you feel that way?"
"Is there a reason why you didn't get to it today?"
"What caused you to say that?"
"Did something happen that made you upset?"
"What would you like to have happened instead?"

TAKE NOTE
In the field of mediation, gathering facts and information about a person's intent is called moving a person from his or her *position* (e.g., I don't want to waste money on a vacation) to the underlying *interest* (I want to save money to help pay for our son to go to college).

Step #3: Report Your Findings and Share Your Point of View

Once you've succeeded at being a detective, the next step is to report your findings. First, you repeat your mate's words back to him or her by summarizing what you heard. This shows that you understand. Then you check in by asking, "Is that right?" For example, "You said that you're upset because when I went to the golf club this morning I told you I'd be home before lunch, but instead I came home after lunch. To you, that meant that I preferred being with my friends over you, is that right?"

If your mate says, "Yes, and . . . ," then listen to the rest of the explanation and rephrase your summary to include all of your partner's points. A good detective wants to be 100 percent accurate in assessing the situation. Taking the time to fully understand your mate's point of view in the disagreement is a powerful sign of respect that can snuff out much of the anger that leads to bad fights. Once you're sure you understand your partner's point of view, express your own. Be clear about what you need and want, why you're hurt, etc., without cursing or blaming. Use language like "When that happened, I was angry because . . . " Take a moment to think out loud about how your perspective and your mate's perspective can coexist. For example, you might be angry because your mate didn't come home for lunch one Saturday, but is it possible that you didn't make it clear that you were looking forward to having lunch together that day? Or perhaps your anger flares because your mate is rude to your father, yet you never considered that your mate's rudeness was in response to negative comments your father has made about your mate. Whatever the situation, you don't have to agree with your partner's perspective, but you do have to

accept the fact that two intelligent people can hold two different views concerning the same event. That is a powerful insight
that keeps you moving forward in a good fight.

Step #4: Partner Up

Once both viewpoints have been shared, it's time to team up and
find a joint solution. Encourage your mate to share some ideas
about how to prevent the same thing from arising again. Regarding the lunch example mentioned previously, you could agree that
you'll be home to have lunch with your mate on the weekend
unless there's a special event. Or perhaps you agree that each of
you will plan separate activities on one weekend day and spend
the afternoon together on the other day. The point here is that you
need to share ideas. Then you must abandon your own idea in
favor of a joint solution that includes a bit of both of your ideas.

HAVE YOU HEARD?
Research on mediation proves that people are more likely to accept
and comply with a solution if they participate in creating it.

Josh and Wendy Use the 5-Minute Conversation

Let's meet Josh, who was my client, and his wife, Wendy, who was
not, and find out how they successfully handled a potential bad
fight by using the 5-minute anticonflict conversation. Note that
Josh is the one who came to me because he couldn't stand fighting with his wife anymore. Once he learned the technique, he
took responsibility for guiding the conversation and keeping it on

the good fight track. He shared his experience with me, and now I share it with you.

Josh Keeps His Cool

It was Wednesday evening, and Wendy and Josh had just gotten home from work. As they prepared the table for dinner, Josh mentioned to Wendy that he had invited his parents over for dinner that Friday night.

Wendy slammed down the plate she was holding. "What? I can't believe you did that without asking me. You're so selfish!"

Alert! Alert! Josh realized that he was about to get into an emotional brawl. He wanted to tell Wendy that he had every right to ask his parents over because he and Wendy spend much more time with her parents than with his, but he didn't say this. He knew that broadening the fight with more topics would make it impossible to solve the immediate problem. He also knew that defending himself would start up a loud shouting match and one of them would end up fleeing to another room. So instead, he said, "Wendy, I'd like to have a 5-minute conversation with you." This might sound awkward, but Josh knew he would much rather have a little awkwardness than enter the battlefield. So he took a seat and asked Wendy to please sit down too.

TAKE NOTE

Your mate is used to bad fights and will try to rope you into one. If your mate verbally counterattacks or twists your words, stay cool and *don't* take the bait.

Josh Becomes a Detective

"Wendy, why are you so mad about this?" he asked.

Wendy was quick to respond: "Why am I mad? Isn't it obvious? You just do whatever you want without thinking about what's good for me."

Josh wanted to fire back with examples of things *she* did that weren't good for *him,* but that wasn't the point here. He could be assertive about those things at another time when they were relevant to the conversation. Right now he needed to focus on the problem created by inviting his parents over. Bringing up anything else would start a snowball conflict. So, instead, he asked another neutral question. "Why would you think that I don't care about what's good for you?"

"You always make decisions for both of us. Did you ever think that I might not want them to come over on Friday?"

Now he thought about the times that *she'd* invited people over without checking with him, but he kept those thoughts to himself and asked a third neutral question that further investigated her anger.

"It's true, I shouldn't make all the decisions, but why is it such a problem to have my parents over?"

"It has nothing to do with your parents. It's just that I'm usually tired on Friday after working all week. You should know that by now. You asked them over without talking to me about it. That's just rude. It's my house and my time too."

He wanted to tell her about his own busy workweek and how getting together with his family was a nice, relaxing thing to do, but he didn't say this because he had committed himself to using the 5-minute conversation to solve this one specific problem (his parents' Friday night visit) and not create additional ones.

As Josh thought about Wendy's response to his neutral questions, he understood the hidden issue. It wasn't that Wendy didn't want to see his parents. She actually likes his parents. She was angry because he made plans for her and the family on the spur of the moment without talking to her first, and that made her feel disrespected.

TAKE NOTE

There is often a hidden reason why someone is mad at you. Find it.

Josh Summarizes His Findings and Shares His Perspective

"Since we haven't seen my parents for a while, I thought having them over Friday night would be a nice, low-key way to visit with them. But I think I get it now. You're upset because you wanted me to talk to you first, before inviting them over. Is that right?"

"If you had asked me, I would have said no, especially this week because I'm extra busy at work," replied Wendy, who was calmer now.

Josh rephrased his summary to include her additional point. "So, you would have said no this week. But it seems like what you really want is for me to talk to you before I make plans for us. Is that right?"

"You got it. Duh," Wendy said, agreeing with the summary.

When Josh shared information in a nonconfrontational way, Wendy was prompted to move out of the war zone and into the listening zone. In a good fight, people pay attention to what the other person is saying and alter their thinking based on what they hear. In a bad fight, no one listens and everyone talks, so resolving the conflict becomes an impossible task.

TAKE NOTE

When you repeat someone's words to him or her, it shows understanding and cools tempers.

Josh Partners Up

Josh offers an option: "Let's figure out what we can do. I could cancel dinner with them and set it up for another time that works for all of us. Should I do that?"

Wendy offers an option: "No, let's not cancel since you already invited them. Let them come, but I'm not cooking. You take care of the food."

Josh presents a solution: "Okay, how about if I order in Chinese food? And what if we say that in the future, we won't make plans unless we talk about it first. How does that sound?"

Wendy responds: "Okay, let's do that."

Josh concludes: "Great. I'm glad we'll get to see my parents, and I'm happy you feel better about it."

I praised Josh for keeping his cool in this discussion. How did he do it? He was prepared and confident in knowing that as long as he stayed focused and followed the steps of the 5-minute anticonflict conversation, he would avoid a blowup and uncover a solution to this problem.

When we know what we should say and have a plan for saying it, we become empowered to avoid the triggers that propel us into emotional frenzies.

Josh handled the situation with such skill that he and Wendy bypassed a broader and meaner snowball fight about: (1) whether Josh is selfish or justified in his actions and whether or not he respects Wendy, (2) whose parents they spend more time with, (3) whether Wendy has ever invited people over unannounced, and (4) whether or not Josh should know that Wendy is tired on Friday nights. Instead of having a major bad fight, they came up with a useful agreement.

TAKE NOTE

When the resolution is reached, express satisfaction with the results.

Get Off the Verbal Merry-Go-Round

When you use this 5-minute anticonflict conversation, what you accomplish will feel like a miracle. No matter what the issue is, you and your mate will be able to move forward and find a solution with respect and consideration for each other. It may take a few times to get it just right, but the more you try, the better you'll get. Take a moment to look back at this chapter and review the steps if you get off track. Soon enough this conversation will become your next best friend—after your partner, of course.

PART THREE

CHANGE YOUR THINKING, NOT YOUR PARTNER

PRACTICE OPTIMISM: FUEL YOUR RELATIONSHIP

Reporter: How does it feel to become a millionaire?

Millionaire: Sad, because I am not a billionaire.

—ANONYMOUS

NOW THAT YOU'VE read Part Two and learned the 5-minute conversations and strategies to fight less and love more, you are wiser, more confident, and prepared to move your relationship to a whole new level. But whether or not you arrive at that level depends on one more factor—your mind-set.

Do you view your relationship through the lens of an optimist or a pessimist? Are you a person who more often says, "Well, that didn't work, let me try again," and proceeds, or are you more inclined to say, "I give up!" when a 5-minute conversation doesn't work the first time? Optimism is the spirit that fuels a relationship during its lows and keeps it strong during its highs.

Could a pessimistic mind-set be blocking you and your partner from achieving the joy and happiness you both deserve? Let's find out.

The Pessimist: If You Think You Can't, You Won't

If you believe that you and your partner can't defy the odds of a divorce or breakup, or that other couples are luckier in love than you are, or that you married a jerk, or that your relationship can't be fixed unless your partner changes first, then expect those negative beliefs to become your reality. This pessimistic attitude will prevent you from reaping the benefits of the lessons, insights, and 5-minute conversations presented in this book. The moment you are frustrated by a conversation with your mate or startled by your mate's antagonism, you will abandon ship. Anytime you face a relationship obstacle, you won't have the conviction to persevere, and, as a result, you won't see the improvements you'd hoped for. You won't be living the life you want; instead, you'll be regretting the life you have.

The Optimist: If You Think You Can, You Will

On the other hand, if you are hopeful and committed to fighting less and loving more, then you'll be motivated to take action and push through the rough waters to calmer seas. By viewing obstacles as movable objects that *all* loving couples experience, you will find smart ways to handle these challenges and move around them. If one way doesn't work, you will try something else. By the way, anyone who claims that her relationship is free of obstacles is either in her first year of couplehood or is flat-out lying—and that's an obstacle!

Whether the obstacle you and your partner face is an argument you've had dozens of times, a hurtful remark that capitalizes on a sore spot, loss of physical intimacy, or one partner's disregard for something that matters deeply to the other, the mind-set with which you choose to react to these issues can make them opportunities for growth or excuses for defeat. It's your choice.

Optimism Is No Fairy Tale

My private practice is filled with couples who come to see me after years of wishing for a miracle to improve their relationship. Some have been in and out of therapy, others have tried periods of separation, but nearly all are waiting for the magical day when they wake up next to one another and once again hear the birds chirping, see the sun shining, and feel the romance they once felt. Some of them tell me that they are optimistic that their relationship can be repaired. They explain that the miracle they are hoping for hasn't yet happened because of the inadequacies and faults of their partners. They are shocked when I burst their bubble and say, "That's not optimism! That's believing in a fairy tale." Optimism means maintaining a positive outlook and taking *action* to turn your hopes and dreams into reality. Putting the burden of action on your mate and hoping that he or she will change won't get you anywhere.

I've worked with many couples who have improved the quality of their relationships through learning new communication skills, gaining mental focus, and adopting an optimistic attitude.

I guarantee that you can enjoy that same outcome if you implement the verbal techniques in this book and embrace an uplifting attitude of faith and optimism. I ask you to turn to your partner at an appropriate time today and share a little optimism: Tell him or her, "I am so glad we are together. Whatever problems we are facing, we are going to work it out. I love you and I believe in us. I want you to know that."

What Kind of Person Are You?

A wise person once said, there are three kinds of people in this world.

1. Those who make things happen
2. Those who watch things happen
3. Those who wonder, "What happened?"

How would you describe your involvement in your relationship? Do you stand by and watch as bad habits consume your relationship? Or are you the kind of person who wants to learn new ways to improve your communication and your relationship? Are you willing to accept the responsibility to be the first to change: the first to apologize, or kiss your partner hello, or offer praise? Optimistic people are not passive, and they don't pass their time waiting for happiness to strike. They are assertive, and they know that happiness is a choice. Optimistic people know that each and every day they must say and do little things to snuff out bad habits and establish good ones.

No matter what kind of a person you are now, you can begin to embrace optimism by implementing the five strategies described on the next page.

Five Strategies to Practice Optimism

Example is not the main thing influencing others. It is the only thing.
                                        —ALBERT SCHWEITZER

1. Choose Your Friends Wisely

For years, Saturday Night Live featured a recurring skit about the Needlers, "The Couple That Should Be Divorced." Dan and Sally Needler are always complaining, fighting, or insulting one another in front of others. They are toxic, sapping other people's optimism and draining their energy. If you have the misfortune to know and spend time with a couple like the Needlers, I suggest you distance yourself quickly. Pessimism and optimism are contagious. Surround yourself with people who have positive attitudes about life and love.

2. Talk Nice to Yourself

Contrary to what you might think, optimists don't think only sunny thoughts 24 hours a day. Many optimists are also realists. They have negative thoughts like anyone else—they just don't let those thoughts go unchallenged. For example, if you're thinking negatively, "What if I don't get the job?" also ask yourself the opposite, positive question, "What if I *do* get the job?" Listen to your answers. If you're upset because your partner forgot to bring you something you need, ask yourself, "Is there another way to get this item? Does it really matter if I have to wait a little while? Have I forgotten to do similar things in the past?" and demand honest answers from yourself. Balancing a negative thought with a positive thought is a mindful way to put yourself in a better mood.

3. Target Mini-Goals

If you aim for nothing, you will surely get that. But if you aim for everything, you will also fail. Once when I was attending a conference, I met a woman who approached me before I was about to present a workshop. She told me she had "tried everything" with her husband, but her relationship was still a mess and she hoped my workshop would help her. I asked her what her goal was. She looked confused and said, "To have a good relationship, of course." Then I asked her, "Well, if you had a good relationship, what would you specifically say and do on a daily basis to reflect this?" She was stumped.

What this woman didn't understand was that vague, end-game goals are tough to achieve. Mini-goals, which are small and specific, are more easily attained and will lead you closer to your big-picture goal incrementally. For instance, you might create a mini-goal to greet your partner with a hug or warm hello every day, or aim to install the five relationship vitals discussed in Chapter 3. Surely, these goals can be easily accomplished, and when they are, you will be inspired to tackle more mini-goals. Success breeds success.

4. Celebrate Your Mini-Successes

While the pessimist looks for what's wrong with a situation, the optimist acknowledges what's wrong, but also makes a conscious effort to spotlight the many little things that are right. Make it a new habit to identify and highlight mini-successes between you and your mate. For instance, if you and your partner fight a lot but were much more civil on a recent day, point it out: "Hey, did you notice that we didn't argue today? I really enjoyed spending time with you." Or if your mate made a generous offer to accompany you to the doctor, acknowledge it by saying, "That was kind of you to offer to go with me. Your support means a lot." Use the start of dinnertime or bedtime as the moment to ask yourself, "What mini-successes happened to us today?" and share them with your mate. The optimist accepts the notion that a lasting relationship is forever a work in progress, but knows that every little step along the way is worth celebrating.

5. Widen Your Lens

Practicing optimism means finding a variety of things, relationships, and interests that bring you peace, comfort, and joy. Don't make your love relationship the only meaningful thing in your life. Widen your lens and get involved with other positive and fulfilling interests and friendships to complement your relationship with your mate. Do you like to go for walks in the park? Then take some walks by yourself. Do you enjoy crafts, sports, yoga, or cooking? Join or start a club or community group. Do you have close friends who make you feel valued and appreciated? Spend time with them. Do you like to write or read? Join an online book group. Do you enjoy spending time with other family members? Reach out to them. Do you take pleasure in spending time with your children? Take them to a museum. Expecting your mate to be your one and only mental, physical, and spiritual connection to the world is a bad idea, because no one person can fulfill every one of your needs.

Optimism Becomes You

As you become more optimistic, you'll also notice that you become more confident. Your determination and commitment to following through with your goals will increase. You'll enjoy other life-changing benefits as well.

Your Likability Improves

Imagine this scenario: You look across the street and see someone you don't like. This person always complains about his or her problems and hardships. What do you do? You instinctively duck into a store, or you stare at the pavement, hoping he or she won't see you. You pretty much do anything and everything to prevent yourself from having to engage with that person.

On the other hand, let's say you see across the street someone who is generally happy, generous, and appreciative. She's someone who has ideas, energy, and enthusiasm for whatever is going on in her life and in yours. Now what do you do? You yell out a welcoming hello. You might even cross the street to initiate a conversation.

When you started dating your mate, you probably expressed a positive attitude about life and your future together. That optimism undoubtedly helped create your love connection, but over the years it may have dissipated as life's challenges arose, leaving you feeling disappointed, angry, and jaded. That negative attitude can hijack your entire personality, something that affects not just your relationship with your partner, but also your role as a parent, daughter or son, sibling, co-worker, and friend. You have the opportunity to break the cycle by choosing to be more optimistic.

Your Health and Well-Being Improve

There is another reward for being more optimistic: People who think positively endure less stress and enjoy better health than those who don't. Research shows that optimists handle stressors better because they believe discrepancies between their goals and their current situation will be resolved, so they're less likely to experience defeat-related moods such as shame, depression, and anger. Studies also show that optimism is tied to better physical health, a stronger immune system, and coping more successfully with health challenges. Simply stated, optimism optimizes your life.

Make Good Things Happen

Let's be honest: It's really easy to fall into a pessimistic rut, especially if that's how you've been operating for a long time. Don't expect to ditch this bad habit without making a deliberate, conscious effort to change your thinking.

If becoming an optimist seems like hard work to you, just consider the time and energy you are currently wasting as a pessimist. Isn't it hard being someone who's constantly filled with anxiety, worry, anger, resentment, and fear about the future of your relationship? All that stress puts you in a bad mood, and then you're sure to find more reasons to be upset and stressed. On the other hand, having an optimistic mind-set means you will spend more of your time in a good mood. A positive lens will brighten your days by allowing you to see strengths and assets in your partner, yourself, and your relationship that you may not have noticed before.

When you combine your new communication skills with an optimistic attitude, you'll find that something amazing happens: Your relationship—and your life—will be easier, happier, and better than ever.

19

YOU: THE GREAT PARTNER

Congratulations! You've completed the *Fight Less, Love More* program and you are fully equipped to transform yourself and your relationship. Whether you know it or not, your training started on the day you purchased this book and began reading it.

You've taken great strides toward building a better life and a better relationship. You've awakened powerful qualities in yourself that will spark optimism, understanding, and love between you and your partner.

So what are these powerful qualities that you now possess? Let's look at the new you, up close and personal.

You Now Possess:

Courage

You have the ability to navigate dangerous waters in search of a better relationship and a better life. You know that you risk a breakup when you bring real issues to the table and open the lines of communication. But you take the chance because you recognize that the only thing you have to lose is your unhappiness.

Knowledge

You understand how your words can single-handedly set off a ripple effect to make things better or worse. You know that you don't have to talk more to improve your relationship; you just have to talk better. You're equipped to reawaken the five love conditions: appreciation, respect, compassion, trust, and companionship. You keep the 5-minute strategies in the back of your mind, knowing that you can use them as needed to resolve conflict.

Self-Control

You recognize the value of exercising self-control to prevent conflict; that's why you hold your tongue and consider your words *before* you open your mouth. With the knowledge of the 5-minute conversations, you can temper your emotions and use logic to change your relationship without blowing up or giving in.

Humility

You don't think you have all the answers; in fact, you know you don't. You listen and encourage your mate to contribute to your conversations. You allow new information to alter your opinions. You admit when you're wrong, and you apologize willingly, recognizing that a perfect apology is another opportunity to build a loving connection through tolerance and understanding.

Confidence

You have more than a dream of a better relationship—you have new information, wisdom, and a practical plan of action for turning that dream into reality. Your feelings of helplessness have been replaced by confidence in your ability to transform your relationship into a love story with a happy ending.

Because you now possess all of these incredible qualities, you are primed to bring out the best in yourself and your partner. You are prepared to breathe life back into your relationship, one conversation at a time.

❦ ❦ ❦

My Friends:
Seize the day!
You are empowered.
You are ready to go the distance.
Stay focused and
You will love more!

With my warmest wishes,
                Laurie Puhn

ACKNOWLEDGMENTS

SPECIAL WORDS OF appreciation go to my mother, Ellen—my collaborator on this book. It is impossible to overstate her contribution. From the book's initial creation to editing, revising, and lastly, to marketing and publicity, she has stood by me with support and feedback and offered reassurance in times of need, keeping my energy strong and my written words flowing. Her belief in the cliché "Where there's a will, there's a way" has been a guiding force in my life.

With great respect, I want to thank my extraordinary agent, Andrea Barzvi of International Creative Management, who helped bring this book to fruition. Her hands-on involvement, encouragement, and business savvy were indispensible. I am grateful to Julie Will, my editor at Rodale, for believing in this endeavor every step of the way. Your edits, enthusiasm, and suggestions made my words sing! Thank you to Jeannie Kim, for providing valuable insights, edits, and comments that raised this book to a higher level.

To my wonderful husband, Dave, I want to express my deepest gratitude for encouraging me to use our relationship as an example in this book, for offering suggestions on the manuscript, and mostly for loving me and showing it every day. I am also grateful to my father, Howard, and sister, Jennifer, for their constant support and belief in this book, as well as for giving me honest feedback and helpful suggestions on the manuscript.

Lastly, these acknowledgments would never be complete without thanking my mediation clients, whose experiences and willingness to share their vulnerabilities allowed me to explore the new and unknown to write this book. While all names have been changed, your stories ring true to anyone who is fighting too much and loving too little. My hope is that the experiences you've shared with me in my office will provide a rich source of material to inspire others to believe that love can last a lifetime.

REFERENCES

Anonymous. 2008. Survey results: The truth about American marriage. *Parade,* September 15. http://www.parade.com/hot-topics/2008/09/truth-about-american-marriage-poll-results.

Atkins, David C., Donald H. Baucom, and Neil S. Jacobson. 2001. Understanding infidelity: Correlates in a national random sample. *Journal of Family Psychology* 15(4): 735–49.

Bramlett, Matthew D., and William D. Mosher. 2001. First marriage dissolution, divorce, and remarriage: United States. *Advance Data from Vital and Health Statistics,* no. 323, May 31. Hyattsville, MD: National Center for Health Statistics.

Bureau of Labor Statistics. 2006. *Women in the labor force: A databook.* Report 996. Washington, DC: US Department of Labor.

Chapman, Gary. 1995. *The five love languages: How to express heartfelt commitment to your mate.* 2nd ed. Chicago: Northfield.

Cohany, Sharon R., and Emy Sok. 2007. Trends in labor force participation of married mothers of infants. *Monthly Labor Review* 130(2): 9–16.

DeAngelis, Tori. 2004. Too many choices? *Monitor on Psychology* 25(6): 56.

Doss, Brian D., Galena K. Rhoades, Scott M. Stanley, and Howard J. Markman. 2009. The effect of the transition to parenthood on relationship quality: An 8-year prospective study. *Journal of Personality and Social Psychology* 96(3): 601–19.

Fisher, Roger, William Ury, and Bruce Patton. 1991. *Getting to yes: Negotiating agreement without giving in.* 2nd ed. New York: Penguin.

Gottman, John M. 1999. *The marriage clinic: A scientifically-based marital therapy.* New York: W. W. Norton.

Gottman, John M., and Nan Silver. 1999. *The seven principles for making marriage work.* New York: Crown.

Grote, Nancy K., and Margaret S. Clark. 2001. Perceiving unfairness in the family: Cause or consequence of marital distress? *Journal of Personality and Social Psychology* 80(2): 281–93.

Hendrix, Harville. 2008. *Getting the love you want: A guide for couples.* 20th anniversary ed. New York: H. Holt.

Janus, Samuel S., and Cynthia L. Janus. 1993. *The Janus report on sexual behavior.* New York: Wiley.

Keim, Brandon. 2007. It's official: Men talk more than women. Wired.com, November 9. http://www.wired.com/wiredscience/2007/11/its-official-me.

Langer, Gary, Cheryl Arnedt, and Dalia Sussman. 2004. Poll: American sex survey: A peek beneath the sheets. ABCNews.com, October 21. http://abcnews.go.com/Primetime/PollVault/story?id=156921&page=1.

Leaper, Campbell, and Melanie M. Ayres. 2007. A meta-analytic review of gender variations in adults' language use: Talkativeness, affiliative speech, and assertive speech. *Personality and Social Psychology Review* 11(4): 328–63.

McEwen, Craig A., and Richard J. Maiman. 1981. Small claims mediation in Maine: An empirical assessment. *Maine Law Review* 33: 237–68.

McGraw, Phillip C. 2000. *Relationship rescue.* New York: Hyperion.

Miller, Courtney Waite, and Michael E. Roloff. 2006. The perceived characteristics of irresolvable, resolvable and resolved intimate conflicts: Is there evidence of intractability? *International Journal of Conflict Management* 17(4): 291–315.

O'Hanlon, Bill. 2000. *Do one thing different: Ten simple ways to change your life.* New York: Harper Paperbacks.

Peters, Mark. 2007. The math on Miss Motor Mouth. PsychologyToday.com, March 1. http://www.psychologytoday.com/articles/200703/the-math-miss-motor-mouth.

Popenoe, David. 2007. The future of marriage in America. *The state of our unions 2007: The social health of marriage in America.* Piscataway, NJ: National Marriage Project, Rutgers, The State University of New Jersey. http://www.virginia.edu/marriageproject/pdfs/SOOU2007.pdf.

Previti, Denise, and Paul R. Amato. 2004. Is infidelity a cause or a consequence of poor marital quality? *Journal of Social and Personal Relationships* 21(2): 217–30.

Puhn, Laurie. n.d. Are babies bad for relationships? ExpectingWords.com. http://expectingwords.com/are-babies-bad-for-relationships.

Rogers, Stacy J., and Paul R. Amato. 1997. Is marital quality declining? The evidence from two generations. *Social Forces* 75(3): 1089–100.

———. 2000. Have changes in gender relations affected marital quality? *Social Forces* 79(2): 731–53.

Ronan, Courtney. 1999. Divvying up those dreaded household chores. *Realty Times,* June 16. http://realtytimes.com/rtpages/19990616_chores.htm.

Schwartz, Barry. 2004. *The paradox of choice: Why more is less.* New York: HarperCollins.

Segerstrom, Suzanne C., Shelley E. Taylor, Margaret E. Kemeny, and John L. Fahey. 1998. Optimism is associated with mood, coping and immune change in response to stress. *Journal of Personality and Social Psychology* 74(6): 1646–55.

Skomal, Lenore. 2008. Are you headed for a split? Five signs your marriage may be in trouble. Womensday.com, September 16. http://www.womansday.com/Articles/Family-Lifestyle/Relationships/Are-You-Headed-for-a-Split.html.

Vaughan, Peggy. 2010. *To have and to hold.* New York: New Market Press.

Weaver, Jane. 2007. Many cheat for a thrill, more stay true for love: MSNBC.com/iVillage survey shows fidelity can be a tough promise to keep. MSNBC.com, April 16. http://www.msnbc.msn.com/id/17951664/ns/health-sexual_health.

World Science Staff. 2009. Do women really talk more than men? *World Science,* April 29. http://www.world-science.net/othernews/070705_gender-talk.htm.

For information about the author, her presentations, and workshops and to receive her free newsletter, go to www.lauriepuhn.com.

INDEX